June Whitfield
At a Glance

June Whitfield

An Absolutely Fabulous Life

Whitfield At a Glance

WEIDENFELD & NICOLSON

Contents

Introduction

My autobiography was published nearly ten years ago. This Weidenfeld & Nicolson epic is a visual portrait of my life and work over the past eighty-four years. Hence the title, *June Whitfield, At a Glance*.

As you can see, I have gone from wigs and glasses and many changes of costume through the decades to eventually appearing as myself and in my later years a couple of dying roles. I have enjoyed working with many comics, so many that my good friend Roy Hudd christened me 'the comics' tart' – thanks, Roy.

There is no censorship now – absolutely anything goes. In the 1950s religion, politics and sex were taboo subjects on BBC radio comedy. Yet writers like Frank Muir and Denis Norden, Alan Simpson and Ray Galton still managed to make millions laugh without resort to swear words or using bodily functions as the basis for their comedy. Things have certainly changed, to the disappointment of many listeners and viewers who miss the gentle and witty humour of earlier days. I wonder what comes next?

My publisher Michael Dover made endless trips to the top of the house to collect the many photo albums and scrapbooks stored there, roughly 60 of them. We have together sorted them out and chosen over 300 photos for the book. My job was to write some hopefully interesting words about each one. My thanks also to Ben Buchan who has spent hours keeping me on the right track and making sure that I haven't written the same thing twice.

I sincerely hope that you will have as much fun flicking through the pages as I have had remembering the days gone by. My apologies to my fellow 'thesps' if I have, in a senior moment, unwittingly omitted them from my story. Happy browsing.

June Whitfield

June Whitfield
Wimbledon, May 2009

Chapter One
GROWING UP

My Communal Family

I was born in Streatham in south London
in November 1925. When I was about two
we moved to a large Victorian house,
'Calderwood', in Palace Road. My mother's
parents Granny and Grandad Flett (above
right), Granny's sister Auntie B (above and left, as a
nurse) and Uncle Billy (above left) all lived with Mum, Dad,
brother John and me at Calderwood. Uncle Billy – Dr Moore
– a doctor in the Medical Corps, met Auntie B when she was
a nurse in the First World War. After they had both died I
learned that although she was known as Mrs Moore they
had never actually been married. Quite scandalous in the
twenties and thirties!

Preceding pages: My parents John (always known as 'Jack')
Whitfield and Bertha Flett on their wedding day, 1 June 1921.
The small picture of me was taken as a formal portrait by the
fashionable photographer Lenare. I hated the fuss.

'Don't buy
anything you
can't afford'

Dad

Dad's father had started a company called Dictograph Telephones in
Yorkshire, which expanded rapidly. Dad came to London and started
as an office boy at the Croydon office. He rose to Managing Director.
I still have some of the official writing paper and a picture of his office
equipped with the latest telephonic equipment. He was liked by all who
worked for him. A wonderful father, he was a very sociable man and
protective of his family. He taught me that money doesn't grow on trees.
He would *never* have had a credit card – he was generous but, true to his
Yorkshire roots, he needed to know where the money went, down to the
last farthing. I loved him dearly.

Mum ('Muff')

Mum was christened Bertha Georgina Flett and known
to her friends as 'Georgie' and to her family as 'Muff'.
She would have loved to have been a professional actress
but her father wouldn't allow it. After her marriage, she
joined amateur dramatic companies and gave brilliant
performances, and was a good director too. My Dad
adored her, we all did. She was glamorous and great fun.

Parents Who Loved Dressing Up

My parents enjoyed cruises, which always included a fancy dress party. In the days when you travelled with trunks full of clothes for every occasion, there were plenty of porters to handle the luggage. These pictures show typical fancy dress competitions: (above) Dad as 'Old Mother Riley' or perhaps 'Charley's Aunt'; (above right) Mum, on the left, in glam mode with fellow travellers and (below right) Dad, on the left, as an eighteenth-century grandee. Muff often won the first prize. She was a leading light of the old-established Comedy Club which performed in the now-demolished Cripplegate Theatre in the City. Dad was also involved.

At Home in Streatham

Calderwood was a Victorian eight-bedroom house. In the big bay window on the first floor (pictured opposite) was Granny and Grandad's bedroom. Mine was the next window to the right, and Mum and Dad's overlooked the tennis court at the side of the house in the picture below. The tennis court was a favourite playground, where once – showing off – I nearly broke my nose doing head-over-heels. I still have the scar. We lived at Calderwood until after the war when my parents sold the house to the Church Commissioners as a home for unmarried mothers. It's now a block of flats. We then moved to Cadogan Place in central London.

The photo below is of Mother, John and me at our first home in Streatham.

Beached

We always spent our summers by the seaside in West Sussex – my favourite county – at first at Felpham, near Bognor, and later at Rosemary Cottage (above), Middleton-on-Sea. Muff and I and John would go for the school holidays, with Dad joining us for the weekends. Whenever we could we spent the days on the beach, which is very stony and I always hated the pebbles (see me in the bottom right picture – the torturous crawl!) A particular memory was the Wall's Ice Cream man and his penny water-ices in triangular cardboard, so cooling on hot days.

My Brother John

John is three and a half years older and, as children, I was the nuisance girl – if he was doing his homework and I interrupted, he threw a cushion at me. I was not wanted. He had a boys' gang and they didn't want girls (below left, I am the little one, trying to be one of the boys). He joined the Army and, after the war, the Foreign Office. His passion was golf. He became Secretary and Captain at Sunningdale, wrote a book about the club's history and was made an honorary member. We are now best friends.

(Opposite) John with his wonderful and talented wife Rosemary ('Bud') on their wedding day. (Opposite below) John in army uniform and John with Dad.

Three Generations

My Dad died when he was 61 after a series of strokes. During the war he went to the office every day and in the evening he was an air raid warden. He seemed to work nearly 24 hours a day and I'm sure that contributed to his relatively early death.

I will always regret that I never took the opportunity to have grown-up discussions with him. I'm sure many people feel the same way when they lose their parents and it is too late to thank them for all they have done. I hope Mum and Dad both knew how much I owe to them.

(Above) Three generations: Muff, me and my greatest achievement, my dearest daughter Suzy, the actress Suzy Aitchison. She is married to Terry. Terry is Irish and has a large family and I have been accepted as a family member. I have a fantastic daughter and a loving son-in-law. How lucky am I.

Chapter Two
THE
DANCING
YEARS

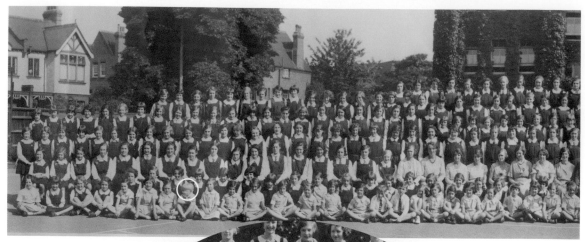

STREATHAM HILL HIGH SCHOOL (G.P.D.S.T.)

July, 1933.

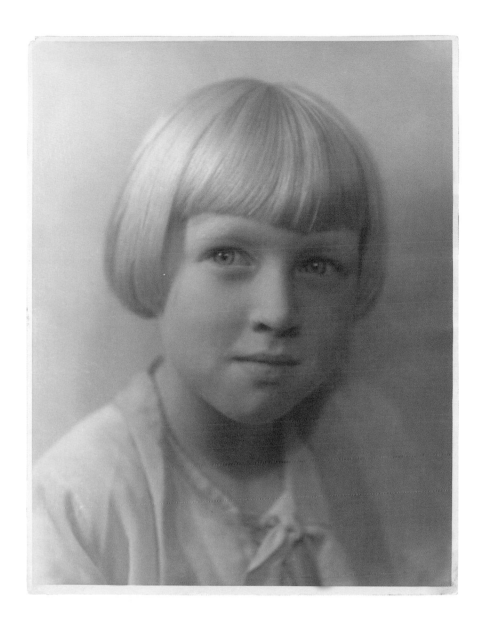

Schooldays

My mother had been a pupil at Streatham Hill High School before me. Here I am in the top photo, eight from the left in the front row, circled, the only girl looking the wrong way. I seem to remember doing that quite often at school – gazing out of the window, wondering how soon I could leave for dancing class.

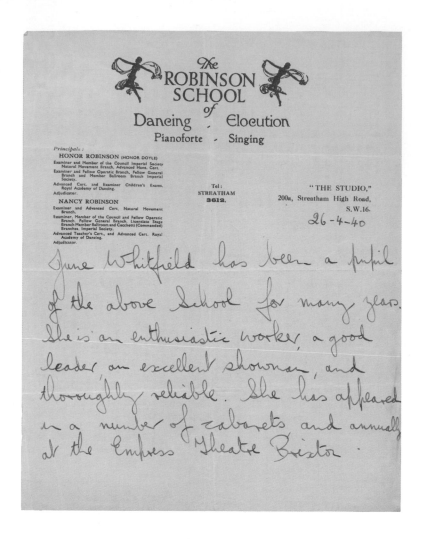

The Robinson
SCHOOL
of
Dancing · Elocution
Pianoforte · Singing

Principals:
HONOR ROBINSON (HONOR DOYLE)
Examiner and Member of the Council Imperial Society
Natural Movement Branch, Advanced Hons. Cert.
Examiner and Fellow Operatic Branch, Fellow General
Branch and Member Ballroom Branch Imperial
Society.
Advanced Cert. and Examiner Children's Exams.
Royal Academy of Dancing.
Adjudicator.

NANCY ROBINSON
Examiner and Advanced Cert. Natural Movement
Branch.
Examiner, Member of the Council and Fellow Operatic
Branch. Fellow General Branch. Licentiate Stage
Branch Member Ballroom and Cecchetti (Commended)
Branches, Imperial Society.
Advanced Teacher's Cert., and Advanced Cert. Royal
Academy of Dancing.
Adjudicator.

Tel:
STREATHAM
3612.

"THE STUDIO,"
200a, Streatham High Road,
S.W.16.

26-4-40

June Whitfield has been a pupil of the above School for many years. She is an enthusiastic worker, a good leader, an excellent showman, and thoroughly reliable. She has appeared in a number of cabarets and annually at the Empress Theatre Brixton.

My Dancing Teacher

(Above) A recommendation to the Royal Academy of
Dramatic Art from my dancing teacher, Miss Nancy Robinson.
My mother would often join the other mothers to watch a class
in progress. Miss Nancy was severe but just, and ticked me
off from time to time. Muff was rather outspoken and said to
her on one occasion: 'June would respond better to a little
encouragement.'

(Opposite) One of many costumes made for me by Gran.

Patterns and materials
were sent out and luckily
for me Gran was great at
dressmaking. But I hated
standing for ages while
she made sure everything
was perfect.

"Here I come, a mini Fred Astaire..."

Stepping Out

(Opposite) Here I come, a mini Fred Astaire...Granny didn't make this one. (Top) Another annual dancing display and (left) a monologue at the Express Theatre, Brixton, in the 1930s.

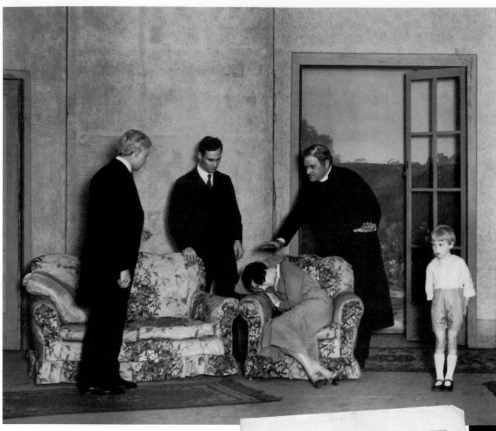

'Am Drams' Again

A non-speaking role, aged five and a half, as 'A Boy'. I was told to stand still and look worried – not too difficult, as I was!

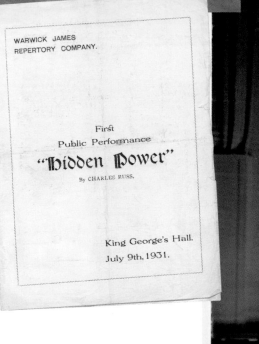

WARWICK JAMES
REPERTORY COMPANY.

First
Public Performance
"Hidden Power"
By CHARLES RUSS.

King George's Hall,
July 9th, 1931.

Puck

Here I am aged nine playing Puck, surrounded by fairies, in Miss Massey's production of *A Midsummer Night's Dream*. Miss Massey taught elocution and acting, with a particular interest in Shakespeare, in a big house on Streatham Common. All her students were in awe of her as she was said to have taught Edith Evans.

78

The Stuart Headlam Shakespeare Association
Instituted 1911
President: SIR JOHNSTON FORBES-ROBERTSON
Chairman: Hon. Sec.:
BERESFORD INGE, Esq., M.A.   HUGH F. SHAW, Esq.

TWO PERFORMANCES OF
SHAKESPEARE'S
A MIDSUMMER
NIGHT'S DREAM
(WITH MENDELSSOHN'S MUSIC)
PRODUCED BY MISS E. C. MASSEY
will be given by
Staff Members of the above Association
on
Saturday, October 26th, 1935
at 2.45 p.m. and 7.45 p.m.
at
KING GEORGE'S HALL
CAROLINE ST., TOTTENHAM COURT ROAD
(Nearest Station, Tottenham Court Road)

PRICES OF ADMISSION:
3/-, 2/-, 1/-.
Numbered, Reserved and Tax Free
Reduction of 25% to parties of 12 at Matinee
Applications for Tickets must be accompanied by remittance and stamped envelope

Hon. Ticket Secretary:
F. W. THORN, Esq., 13, Birchwood Court, Burnt Oak, Edgware
Telephone : COLindale 6111

A. Prudan Printer, 37, High Street, Edgware

"Puck" (June)
Good Luck
Love from Daddy

Most tender Juvenal, my worthy neighbour,
Oh, pray accept, although not good enough,
This gift, the fruit of Mr Lyons' labour,
. . my love, dear Moth,
— your Senior Tough!

. . . . akespeare Association
. 1925
. . . . . FORBES-ROBERTSON
. . . . . Hon. Sec.:
,937   T. A. GILBERT, Esq.

TWO PERFORMANCES OF
SHAKESPEARE'S
LOVE'S LABOUR'S LOST

Produced by Miss E. C. MASSEY, will be given by
Staff Members of the above Association
on
SATURDAY, OCTOBER 30th
at 2.45 p.m. and 7.45 p.m.
at
KING GEORGE'S HALL
CAROLINE STREET, TOTTENHAM COURT RD.
(Nearest Station, Tottenham Court Road)

PRICES OF ADMISSION:

3s., 2s., 1s.   Numbered, Reserved and Tax Free
Reduction of 25% to Parties of 12 at Matinee

Application for Tickets must be accompanied by Remittance and
Stamped Envelope

Hon. Ticket Secretary: F. W. THORN, Esq.,
15, Birchwood Court, Burnt Oak, Edgware
Telephone: COLindale 6111

A. PRUDEN, The Edgware Press, High St., Edgware

See file for Programme MOTH.

A Little Genius

I WENT to see the teachers and instructors of the London County Council's evening institutes do "Love's Labours Lost" for the benefit of their students and saw a little girl of twelve romp away with the honours of the evening.

The performance of June Whitfield as Moth, page to the fantastical Armado, made me wonder if the wise-heads who say that Shakespeare is not for children are right.

She is twelve and is a normal, eager suburban child. She lives at Streatham.

On the stage at King George's Hall she was astonishing in every way—her confidence, her word perfection, her articulation and her zest for the play. Her slight figure in green hose, a silvery doublet, a silver cap with a green feather, left her a child, but her acting placed her above all but two adults.

June has already played Puck in "A Midsummer Night's Dream" and Mamillius in "The Winter's Tale."

The oustanding teachers were Alec Powis as Berowne and Olive Grieg as Rosaline.

Moth

Next came Moth in *Love's Labour's Lost*, with a fairly tiresome and time-taking hair-do – hot tongs, I suspect. Above is the aftermath of the hair-do, with the odd kink left behind. 'A Little Genius'... oh well, nothing lasts for ever.

Pageant Play of
Streatham

Streatham High Road
in the
Eleventh Century

EMB

P R O G R A M M E

formance of Members of the COMEDY CLUB of

"H O U S E M A S T E R"

(a Play in three Acts by Ian Hay)

at Russell School, Ballards,

on Tuesday, 17th January, 1939.

------oOo------

C H A R A C T E R S
(in order of appearance)

CHARLES DONKIN	J.H.WHITFIELD
"BIMBO" FARRINGDON	DICK STICKNEY
VICTOR BEAMISH	E.F.MASTERTON-SMITH
FRANK HASTINGS	J.P.AMIS
ELLEN	MARY SHENTON
BARBARA FANE	HILDA NOLLER
"BUTTON" FARRINGDON	JUNE WHITFIELD
MATRON	MARY PRESTON
ROSEMARY FARRINGDON	JOAN STRETTELL
CHRIS FARRINGDON	BERYL ELLIS
PHILIP DE POURVILLE	PATRICK FEATHERBY
"FLOSSIE" NIGHTINGALE	DOUGLAS BRYCE-GRANT
THE REV. EDMUND OVINGTON	HAROLD HERSEE
SIR BERKELEY NIGHTINGALE	SIDNEY C. NEWTON
TRAVERS	J.F.WHITFIELD
"POP"	NIGEL SANDYS-SMITH
"OLD CRUMP"	LAWRENCE CHRISTIE

SYNOPSIS OF SCENES

A C T   I

Scene 1.   Mr. Donkin's Study - Morning.
Scene 2.   The same - Later in the day.

A C T   II

Scene 1.   The Girls' Bedroom - Three weeks later.
Scene 2.   Mr. Donkin's Study - The following morning.

A C T   III

Mr. Donkin's Study - Three weeks later.

The Play Produced by
BERTHA G. WHITFIELD.

My Best Friend

(Opposite) The *Pageant Play of Streatham* in 1936
was another Miss Massey triumph. I played 'A Sweyne'
and heralded the coming of the monks to Streatham.
Then I played Buttons in *The Housemaster* by Ian Hay.
Directed by my mother, it starred my Dad and even
John was roped in – a real family affair for the
'Comedy Club'.

In 1940 I caught diphtheria, foolishly diving into
a stagnant swimming pool and swallowing a large
gulp of water. After weeks in hospital I spent a couple
of months recuperating on a farm in Devon with my
best friend Margaret Faithful, known as Mog (we had
met years before at dancing school). The photo above
was taken at Felpham during another holiday. We are
still best friends.

Chapter Three
THE WEST END IN WARTIME

Keep Up the Shorthand...

(Above) An attempt to 'vamp it up'. (Bottom right) Years later, when
I excitedly showed Dad a contract for £12 a week – having progressed
from £3 a week – he simply said, 'Well done, but you are keeping up
the shorthand and typing, aren't you?'

Royal Academy of Dramatic Art.

QUALIFYING TEST.

To be held at 62, GOWER STREET, LONDON, W.C. 1

, at

on

The Candidate must learn and speak in character one of the following passages. When the passage has been selected the whole play should be obtained and read through ; the cand date must also be prepared to recite one short piece, verse or prose chosen independently of this list. A copy of the piece of the Candidate's own choice must be brought to the examination.

Shorthand-Typist Certificate

This is to Certify that

JUNE WHITFIELD

has undergone the prescribed examination and has passed a test in Pitman's Shorthand at the rate of

ONE HUNDRED

words a minute

and furnished an accurate Typewritten Transcript of the Shorthand Notes within the prescribed time.

Pitman's Shorthand Institute,
London

2ND JUNE, 1942.

Taught by _____

"PINK STRING & SEALING WAX".

      This is to confirm your engagement as A.S.M. and second Understudy in the above-named Play at a salary of £3 per week. The engagement is to commence tomorrow, April 20th, and is to be subject to a fortnight's notice on either side.

      Yours sincerely,

      (E.P.Clift)

MINISTRY OF LABOUR AND NATIONAL SERVICE.
THE EMPLOYMENT OF WOMEN (CONTROL OF ENGAGEMENT) ORDERS, 1943.

Permit

THE MINISTER OF LABOUR AND NATIONAL SERVICE hereby certifies that until the 23rd day of May 1944 WHITFIELD June Rosemary (Miss) (name in full) of 5 Palace Rd. S.W.2. (address) EMBC 256/3) (national registration identity no.) is exempted from the provisions of the above Order in respect of the employment specified or described below.

EMPLOYMENT TO WHICH THIS PERMIT RELATES.

Actress (Student)

Signed by the order of the Minister of Labour and National Service this 24th day of April 1944

      Manager.
      Local Office.
TOOTING
62 Upper Tooting Rd.
Tooting SW17

E.D. 419 (Revised).

A Close Call

David Horne (centre in the cartoon opposite) taught at RADA and in 1944 he suggested me for the job of assistant stage manager at the Duke of York's Theatre for the Victorian family play *Pink String and Sealing Wax* – my first professional job. The war came very close one night during the play. Just as a meal ended onstage, a bomb fell on nearby St Martin-in-the-Fields, shaking the actors and audience. The next line in the play was: 'For what we have received, may the Lord make us truly thankful.'

(Above) The same play at the Penge Empire, with a change of cast. I was promoted to playing Jessie (I'm on the right).

FIRST VISIT TO THIS THEATRE!

WILLIAM WATT presents

THE FAMOUS RADIO FEATURE

"APPOINTMENT WITH FEAR"

(BY ARRANGEMENT WITH THE B.B.C.)

YOU HAVE HEARD IT ON "THE AIR"—NOW SEE IT ON THE STAGE!

AN EVENING OF SUSPENSE AND THRILLS!!

(BUT WITH NOTHING "HORRIFIC")

Specially written by **JOHN DICKSON CARR** author of the famous
for the stage B.B.C. Plays

WITH THE FAMOUS ACTRESS

ETHEL WARWICK

PERSONAL APPEARANCE OF

LEWIS STRINGER

FROM THE ACTUAL RADIO FEATURE!

(Kindly released by the B.B.C. for this Tour)

YOUR STORY **"THE MAN IN BLACK"**
TELLER—

(As usual the Voice of VALENTINE DYALL)

TWO ABSORBING PLAYS—BOTH IN ONE EV[ENING]

NO. I	"INTRUDING SHADOW" The Author challenges you to solve this Mystery	Staged and Directed by **MARTYN C. WEBSTER** as on the Radio	NO. [2]

Theatre Royal, Bath

22nd MAY 1945

'APPOINTMENT WITH FEAR'

IRENE VANBRUGH HEADS THE CAST

To witness acting of so superlative a character that it positively compels attention is the good fortune of playgoers who visit the Theatre Royal, Bath, this week. There are certainly some novel...

...over-anxious wife.

June Whitfield instantly captures and consistantly retains our sympathy as the girl spy.

Keith Shepherd presents two...

...the fate of a woman spy during the Napoleonic war, and its appeal at the present moment in a sense topical. Of the two plays, the second rises to greater dramatic heights.

Adorns Her Part.

Many of the company give convincing proof of their versatility by appearing in dual roles. Dame Irene Vanbrugh, who ably fulfilled the task of thankfully... appears as the imperious... Lady Stanhope. The role of this courageous and resourceful grande... is one which she is supremely fitted to adorn, and she lives her part inspiringly, convincingly and enthusiastically.

The feminine interest is numerically slight, Barbara Douglas playing convincingly in the earlier play as the victim of the blackmailer, and Namara Michael gives a good study of a dominating and over-anxious wife.

June Whitfield instantly captures and consistantly retains our sympathy as the girl spy.

Keith Shepherd presents two excellent studies as the garrulous George Parsons and the Belgian peasant. The latter is his finer achievement. Lewis Stringer finds the finer of his two opportunities as Capt. Thorpe in the second play. His tragic expression at one crucial moment represents true art.

Frederick Horrey completes the cast of the Napoleonic play by his appropriate study of the brutal German officer.

In the first play, Ian Howard is true to type as the chivalrous police officer and Robert Hey plays well as the valet. The standard of execution is excellent.

L.B.H.

POST OFFICE

TELEGRAM

Office of Origin and Service Instructions.

Prefix. 97 Time handed in.

97 10.0 SOUTH LONDON T 16

[MI]SS JUNE WHITFIELD PALACE THEATRE WESTCLIFFONSEA =

[BE]ST OF LUCK DARLING FROM ALL AT HOME =

LOVE MUSS ++

MUSS +

Girl Spy in Cupboard

(Left) Dame Irene Vanbrugh originally headed the cast of *Appointment With Fear*. It was a privilege and a great learning curve to watch Dame Irene on stage. She was magical.

(Above) With Lewis Stringer. I was a girl spy discovered hiding in a cupboard by a 'baddie'. I had my face slapped once a night and twice on matinee days. I broke out in a rash, so Frederick Horrey gave me a good slap on Mondays and Saturdays and we faked it the rest of the week.

Pickles brings comedy hit home

THERE was a warm welcome for Walter Greenwood's light-hearted Lancashire comedy, "The Cure for Love," at the Opera House, Manchester, last night at the end of a successful 40 weeks' tour.

As Jack Hardacre, returned Eighth Army sergeant, caught in a tangle of Salford love in the private bar of "The Flying Shuttle," Wilfred Pickles had a part that fitted him like a glove.

Of the supporting players, one of the most entertaining was June Whitfield's Salford floosie—Janie Jenkins, a gal of the gum-chewing variety. Ella

POST OFFICE
TELEGRAM
Office of Origin and Service Instructions.

Charges to pay
LS   d.
RECEIVED

Prefix. Time handed in.

72

At
From
By

LS A 139 11.13 SOUTH LONDON T 21

JUNE WHITFIELD CURE FOR LOVE COY THE NEW
THEATRE HULL =

HERES TO YOU DARLING LET IT GO LOVE FROM
ALL = MOTHER +

For free repetition of doubtful words telephone "TELEGRAMS ENQUIRY" or call, with this form,
at office of delivery. Other enquir' should be accompanied by this form, and, if possible, the env

PARKWOOD PRODUCTIONS LTD.

DIRECTORS:
JAMES PARK, J.P., F.C.A.
WALTER GREENWOOD

22, BRIDGE STREET.
MANCHESTER. 3.
BLACKFRIARS 7974.

ans. 3.12.46

Miss June Whitfield.

The Directors of Parkwood Productions Ltd.,

and

The Walt Greenwood Film Unit Ltd.,

would be delighted if you would join a party

at the Queens Hotel, Manchester,

immediately after the last performance of the

play, on Saturday, 14th December, 1946.

R.S.V.P.

The Cure for Love

A ten-month tour of this play with Wilfrid Pickles who was at the height of his popularity with his radio show *Have a Go*. Full houses everywhere and a great cast. Ginny Leslie and I became good friends and we were ticked off by Wilfrid for giggling on stage. We played cards with Wilfrid and Mabel. I lost, and paid my £5 dues (big money then). At Christmas my cheque was returned with a note from Wilfrid, 'Stop sticking on 16.'

STAGE TALK

I HAVE a great admiration for June Whitfield, who plays the part of Janie Jenkins in "The Cure for Love" at the Bradford Prince's Theatre.

For the sake of her art she transforms herself into an unsavoury cotton town Jezebel, and goes on to the stage each evening knowing that not one member of the audience will have a grain of sympathy for her.

To prepare herself for this she wears a wig to hide her own beautiful hair, besmirches her lovely complexion with a liberal layer of rouge, and dons garish slacks. Thus attired she enters the stage with a mouthful of the real Lancashire dialect.

* * *

JUNE WHITFIELD and Virginia Leslie, who plays the billetee, are two charming young actresses who should make headway.

Curiously enough Virginia

has not confined herself to acting either, for in her determination to know all there is to know about the theatre she did a spell of stage-managing of the play, "Fit for Heroes."

FRANCIS LAIDLER'S PANTOMIMES

London Address:
15, Park Mansions,
Knightsbridge, S.W.1
Telephone:
Kensington 2325

All Communications to—
THE ALHAMBRA THEATRE, BRADFORD. (*Telephone* 9650) 21444

Alhambra Theatre, Bradford
24th Sept. 1947

Dear Miss Whitfield,

I have just arranged all details respecting the dates and times of the first rehearsals, probable length of runs, and particulars of matinees in connection with my Bradford and Leeds Pantomimes.

As at present arranged, the First Call for Principals for my "CINDERELLA" Pantomime at the Alhambra Theatre, Bradford, will be at 10 o'clock on Tuesday morning, Dec.9th/1947, and that rehearsal will continue until 1.30 p.m. The next rehearsal will be on the same day at 3.30 until 7 p.m. and I will let you know about all other rehearsals in good time.

The Bradford "Cinderella" Pantomime will be produced on Tuesday, Dec.23rd/1947, and it is expected that it will have a run of 14½ weeks, finishing on Saturday, Apr.3rd, 1948, which is the end of Easter Week.

The performances will be Twice Daily for the first 6½ weeks, until Saturday, Feb.7th/1948. Then for the next 4 weeks (until Sat.Mch.6/48) it is intended that there shall be matinees daily except on Fridays. For the last 4 weeks (until Sat. Apr.3rd/1948) it is intended that there shall be matinees daily except on Mondays and Fridays, but with a Special Matinee on Easter Monday, March 29th/1948

Regards.

Yours faithfully,

F. Laidler.

Miss June Whitfield

The Show Must Go On

The pantomime ran from December 23rd to April 3rd – fourteen and a half weeks including Easter! The winter of 1947 was cold, cold, cold, with deep snow. But the show did go on, with me as Cinderella and Wilfrid Pickles as Buttons. Somehow the entire company and, most importantly, the audience managed to get to the theatre.

Francis Laidler pantomimes were famous in the north
of England. They were always of a high standard,
beautifully dressed and with a full orchestra. In later
years some pantos settled for piano, drums and the
odd violin. We were spoilt!

FAY LENORE
"Prince Charming"

BARBOUR BROS.
"The Broker's Men"

RICHARD MILNER
Ugly Sister "Julia"

THE JOHN TILLER GIRLS

A Carnival of Fun

MARION DAWSON
Ugly Sister "Trixie"

BERT RICH
"Baron de Broke"

JUNE WHITFIELD
"Cinderella"

JUNE CAMPANY
"Dandini"

CINDERELLA'S PONIES

A Superb Spectacle

W. JACKSON

"Cinderella"

(MARION DAWSON)

RICHARD MILNER

"THE UGLY SISTERS" ARE MAN-HATERS — THEY CAN'T GET A MAN — AND THEY HATE IT!

THE BARBOUR BROS. AS "THE BROKER'S MEN" NEED HARD CASH TO GIVE 'EM A SOFT TIME

WILFRED (ARE YOU COURTIN'?) PICKLES "BUTTONS" IS COURTING CINDERS

HOUSE-MAID'S KNEE IS NOT SO ATTRACTIVE AS HOUSE-MAID'S KNEES — ESPECIALLY IF THEY BELONG TO "CINDERS"

JUNE WHITFIELD

WILF'S WIFE MABEL PLAYS "MARGERY"

"DANDINI" JUNE CAMPANY — AND SHE'S THE KIND OF CAMPANY WE'D LIKE TO ASK TO TEA

FAY LENORE PLAYS "THE PRINCE" WHO WANTS CINDERS TO LOVE, HONOUR AND OH, FAY!

ARTHUR FERRIER

"THE BARON" ONCE A RECKLESS YOUNG BLOOD — NOW A BLOODLESS OLD WRECK

BERT RICH

INCOME TAX DEMAND

MONEY FOR JAN!

OUR ARTIST'S SKETCHES OF A FEW OF THE PRINCIPALS APPEARING AT THE THEATRE ROYAL, LEEDS.

June Whitfield (Cinderella) and Fay Lenore (Prince
Charming) in a scene from Francis Laidler's pantomime
"Cinderella," which opened at Bradford Alhambra
Tuesday.

JUNE WHITFIELD,
Cinderella in the Bradford pantomime, pictured
here with Wilfred Pickles.

FRANCIS LAIDLER'S PANTOMIMES

London Address:
15, Park Mansions,
Knightsbridge, S.W.1
Telephone:
Kensington 2325

All Communications to—
THE ALHAMBRA THEATRE, BRADFORD. *(Telephone 9550)*

Alhambra Theatre, Bradford
25th Sept. 1947

Miss June Whitfield,
52 Cadogan Place, S.W.1.

Dear June,

I am sorry I forgot to pay your expenses when you were at Bradford to-day, but I have taken a special note of it and will deal with the matter when I see you next time.

Enclosed herewith are coupons for one pair of Ballroom Shoes, and in due course will you please, when you have purchased the shoes, let me have a Shop's receipt for the coupons, because I have to forward Shops' receipts for all coupons to the Board of Trade. In the meantime you might let me know that you have received the enclosed seven coupons safely. Regards.

Yours sincerely

F. Laidler.

June Whitfield (Cinderella) and Wilfred Pickles (Buttons) are left in the Baron's kitchen on the night of the ball. A scene from Francis Laidler's pantomime "Cinderella," which opens at the Alhambra Theatre, Bradford, on Tuesday next.

No Shoes Without Coupons

Do read this letter from Francis Laidler. I treasure it. It enclosed coupons for Cinderella's ballroom shoes, a reminder that rationing was still with us in 1947. My Dad liked sweets and I liked clothes, so we swapped. Fair swap, I thought. I'd still rather have clothes than sweets.

Chapter Four

LEARNING FROM LEGENDS

Working for the Master

What a fantastic opportunity to work for Noël Coward in his play *Ace of Clubs*. The girls were not 'chorus', we were small part players. We had names and at least one line each. While you were working for 'the Master' you became a member of his family. I was lucky enough to attend parties at Gerald Road and to visit 'Goldenhurst', his country residence, with Hugh Martin and Jack Gray, where we played and sang the score of their musical *Love from Judy*. Coward was undoubtedly a genius.

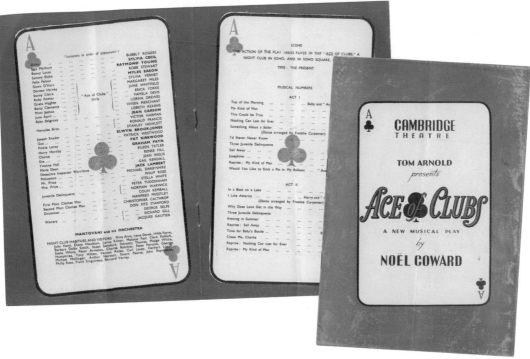

Ace of Clubs was set in a nightclub. (Above) Here we are about to entertain the guests. In another racy number we pranced around with balloons attached, inviting the diners: 'Would you like to stick a pin in my balloon, Daddy?'

(Opposite top) Graham Payn and us girls (me behind his left ear). The beautiful photographs were taken by the celebrated photographer Angus McBean.

Jeanne et Cie Ltd.
26 Rupert St., London, W.1
GERrard 1393

Jolly good luck
and fondest wishes
Graham

For June
from
N.C.

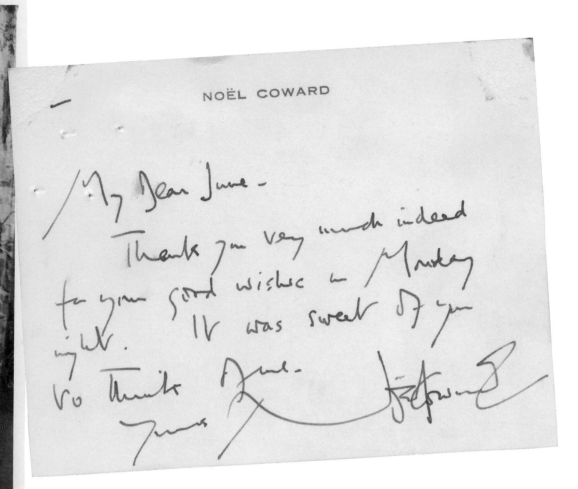

NOËL COWARD

My Dear June –

Thanks you very much indeed for your good wishes on Monday night. It was sweet of you so thanks June.

Yours

[signature]

A Night to Remember

A party in Manchester for the cast of *Ace of Clubs* attended by 'the Master'. In London I was living with my parents. The show arrived at the Cambridge Theatre and, after several months, I invited some of the cast home after the show. I was absolutely thrilled when Graham announced, 'The Master would like to come.' Wow! He turned up with Joyce Cary and Cole Leslie. Mum was overjoyed, Noël played our piano and a good time was had by all.

PENNY PLAIN

ST MARTIN'S THEATRE
WEST STREET
W.C.2.

All Seats Bookable in Advance

PROGRAMME   SIXPE

"PENNY PLAIN"

Owing to the indisposition of
MOYRA FRASER and MARJORIE DUNKELS
their parts at this performance will be played by
DELIA WILLIAMS, NAOMI DUNNING
DAPHNE PERETZ and JUNE WHITFIELD

DANCE and WE BEG TO DIFFER will be cut:
they will be replaced by HANGOVER by and with
RICHARD WARING
and PROBLEMS OF THE MALE DANCER
from Part 2.

To wish, JUNE a lot
more than a Penny-
worth of luck
and a
happy
time

in
'Penny Plain'
from
Joyce
Grenfell

ONE OF THE BEST REVUES IN YEARS

"Penny Plain," which opened at the St. Martin's Theatre last night, is one of the best revues for years.

Another Legend: Joyce Grenfell

Another great cast I was lucky to be part of was Laurier Lister's revue *Penny Plain*. In the photo above – another one taken by Angus McBean – are, from the left: Liz Welch (a wonderful singer and a great card-player), Rose Hill, Delia Williams, Moyra Fraser, Marjorie Dunkels, me, Joyce Grenfell.

Opposite is a first-night note from Joyce, not only a brilliant artist but also a cartoonist.

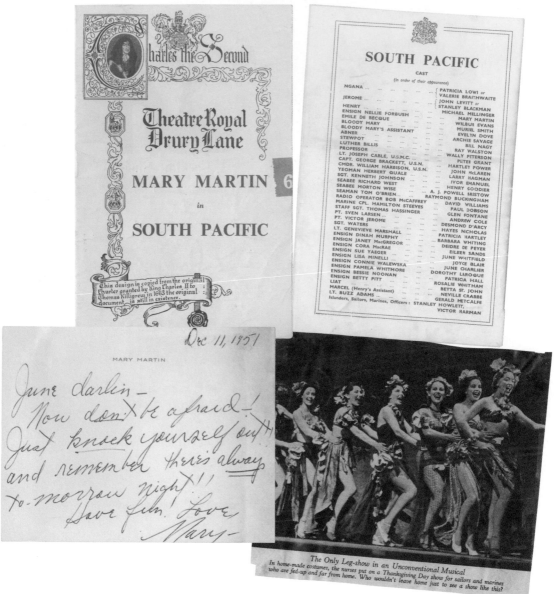

The Only Leg-show in an Unconventional Musical
In home-made costumes, the nurses put on a Thanksgiving Day show for sailors and marines who are fed-up and far from home. Who wouldn't leave home just to see a show like this?

South Pacific

(Above) Leading the girls. We all had to tan for the first London run in 1951 of this famous Broadway musical. One or two of us girls didn't do sun-beds, so we smothered each other in rather thick and smelly tan out of a bottle – very messy but better than being burned. Mary Martin, another superb star, never missed a performance – she'd done 900 shows in New York alone – and every one was like a first night. Her son Larry Hagman, later J.R. Ewing in *Dallas*, was also in the show. We all fancied him.

(Opposite) This photo was taken in 1988 when Mary came over to see the current production and I was privileged to sit with her.

JEAN CARSON

BILL O'CONNOR   JOHNNY BRANDON
JUNE WHITFIELD   LINDA GRAY
AUDREY FREEMAN   WILLIAM GREENE
AND ADELAIDE HALL and Company of 50 Artistes
IN
EMILE LITTLER'S

"LOVE FROM JUDY xxx"

A New Musical

By ERIC MASCHWITZ and JEAN WEBSTER   Music by HUGH MARTIN
Lyrics by HUGH MARTIN and JACK GRAY   Orchestrations by PHILIP GREEN
Choreography by PAULINE GRANT Scenery and Costumes by BERKELEY SUTCLIFFE
DIRECTED BY CHARLES HICKMAN

NOW AT THE SAVILLE THEATRE Temple Bar 4011
EVENINGS at 7-30   SATURDAYS at 5 and 8-20   MATINEE WEDNESDAYS at 2-30

Love from Judy

I had been in New York with *Women of Twilight*, a play which the critics closed after a week, but it enabled me to stay and learn the score of a musical, *Love from Judy,* by Hugh Martin and Jack Gray, in order to demonstrate it to various promoters. Emile Littler eventually presented the show. Jean Carson was the star and I played one of her room-mates, Sally McBride. I had met the authors when I was in *Penny Plain*.

"SALLY McBRIDE"
IN
"LOVE FROM JUDY"

With best wishes to ... from June '80

JUNE WHITFIELD CAPTIVATES

One of the two stars "born" on the first night of the new British musical "Love From Judy," which opened at the Saville Theatre last week, was June Whitfield, daughter of a former Streatham councillor, Mr. J. H. Whitfield.

With her fair hair flowing down her back, June Whitfield, playing Sally McBride—the production is based on "Daddy Long-Legs"—wove a spell over her audience with her dancing and singing.

In the first act she has two fine contrasting numbers, "Dumb-Dumb-Dumb," a playful commentary on dumb blondes, and "Here We Are," a sentimental song.

And at the end the girl, whose previous best was a "bit" part in a Noel Coward musical, received an ovation.

"Love From Judy" tingles with youth, dazzles and delights. The

During the relay of "Love from Judy" from the Saville, with the "sound" being far from co-operative, I was impressed not only by the lead, Jean Carson, who is definitely star material, but by another young English girl, June Whitfield. This show owes much to its delightful music and lyrics by the American Hugh Martin, and Miss Whitfield sang one of his best songs, "Here We Are," with special grace. She has a charming presence and a voice sweet and clear as a bell.

(Top) *Love from Judy* cartoon.
(Above) with Hugh Martin,
composer. (Below left) with
Jack Gray, lyricist.

June steps in
—first for Joy and then for Jean

ise of the biggest part in her career, as a college girl in a new musical, "Love from Judy" (with music by Hugh Martin) based on the famous play

JUNE WHITFIELD

June is ready for biggest part

A thundering theatrical flop across the Atlantic has set a young Kensington actress on the road to success. Blonde, attractive Miss June Whitfield, of Kensington Court, visited New York with a small part in the ill-fated American production of "Women of Twilight" which folded up in seven days.

This part followed a spell at RADA and a tour of several repertory companies culminating in a number of West End parts including one in "South Pacific"—but all on the small side.

While in New York Miss Whitfield met song-writer Hugh Martin, who in turn introduced her to impressario Emile Littler. The result was that June came back to England with the prom-

"Daddy Long Legs." This opens for a prior-to-West-End tour in Coventry next week and comes to London at the end of the month.

Taking Over

I spent many of my earlier years taking over from people. I followed Dora Bryan in the tour of *Cure for Love*, took over from Joy Nichols in the radio series *Take It From Here* – Alma Cogan and I shared the role – and played 'Judy' for some time when Jean Carson was ill. 'Always the bridesmaid, never the bride', but I've enjoyed every moment.

The opening story of *Judy* was 'Mardi Gras', hence the hat. (Below) me on the extreme left in the 'dream ballet'. Barbara Windsor was one of the orphans in this story of another orphan, Judy. I shared a dressing-room with Audrey Freeman, who was being courted by David Tomlinson and later married him.

Grease-Paint on the Mind

MISS WHITFIELD, BECOMING suddenly in voice, gesture and appearance an elderly Civil Servant, produces a sheet of paper from a large reticule. "You will faind here," she says, "all mai vital statistics."

The sheet of paper seems to have been torn from an exercise book. It is covered with writing in green ink. "Some time ago," Miss Whitfield says, returning for a moment to her ordinary voice, "I was compelled to visit the Labour Exchange. Before they could assist me they said they would have to know what I'd been doing in the last five years." Her eyes become the size of saucers. She demonstrates total astonishment. "In the last five years! I had no idea! But then I thought I really ought to know what I had been doing, so I wrote all that down."

"All that," begins with a list of personal details, under the heading of: "Full name; professional name; permanent address; birthday; medals, etc." Under 'medals' appears the note: "Gertrude Lawrence prize (shared)." "One must be honest, must one not?" says Miss Whitfield, turning into the headmistress of a girls' school.

The dossier then branches out into a detailed catalogue of Miss Whitfield's public appearances, ranging from *The Desert Song* to *Focus on Nursing* (B.B.C.), *Devon accent and baby noises.* There is also a note: "Xmas '49; offer from Emile Littler to play Cinderella at People's Palace. Refused (salary offered less than half last year's)."

"You will note," says Miss Whitfield, now apparently a guide on a conducted tour, "my parts in *South Pacific* and that sort of thing, and now let's throw that away and look at this." 'This' is an article in a small radio paper. Miss Whitfield reads out two lines: "June grew up with greasepaint on her mind if not on her features." "I believe," she says, "that the gentleman who wrote that was the one who asked me if I had any hobbies. Hobbies?" The very sound seemed fantastic.

Miss Whitfield has moved into Jean Carson's place in *Love from Judy*, and into Joy Nicholls' place in *Take It From Here.* "I could tell you how I was hired," she says, "but it takes two or three days. For the rest, I live quietly at home in modest luxury with my parents in Cadogan Place. I am, I believe, 28 years of age. Unmarried."

Miss Whitfield, who is about the size of a midget, looks fierce. "What I tell all my gentlemen is this. I'm doing all right the way I am. If I have to get married let's make it a fair swop."

THE
MUSIC MAKER
presents
JUNE
WHITFIELD
The New British Singing Star

Now appearing
in the
London Success
LOVE FROM JUDY
at the
**SAVILLE
THEATRE**

LECT RECORD No. 1
N THIS MUSIC MAKER

ing with Someone
Lonely Days

}

PHILIPS
Record No.
PB 137

JUNE WHITFIELD

Ker Robertson's DISCoveries

ENTER another British disc artist to help stem the U.S. flood—June Whitfield (no relation to the excellent David).

She is 27, blonde and trim, and up to now has made a comfortable living on the stage.

June has come up the orthodox way: R.A.D.A. at 17, assistant stage manager in a London theatre, small straight parts, singing in panto with Wilfred Pickles, West End understudy, revue work and a cabaret spot—and now in the groove.

Can she sing? Yes, pleasingly, and with experience will be a welcome home entertainer. Her first record has *Seven lonely days*, backed by *Dancing with someone* ('78 Philips PB137).

★ The song that comes to us via Tokyo and San Francisco, *Gomen nasai* (which, they say, means "forgive me"), has some charm. Say 5 per cent.

Current praise

Cyril Stapleton's band make the most of it, building up the instrumental effects to aid the thin little melody ('78 Decca F10104).

Harry Belafonte makes it 90 per cent. vocal and unembellished. You takes your choice . . .('78 HMV B10469).

heart-strings taut as violin strings ('78 Columbia DB3285).
★ Vera Lynn's waltz disc, *The Windsor* backed by *The Lambeth*, is shooting up the fame ladder. One-woman-industry V. L. still remains an easygoing charming personality ('78 Decca F10092).

The Wrong Accent

I was persuaded to make a couple of records at this time. Although my voice served me well in musicals and revue, I soon learned that I was not going to be the next Judy Garland. 'Seven Lonely Days' was a Dolly Parton-type song, and my English accent did me no favours.

TAKE IT FROM HERE—With Mr. Dick Bentley, Miss June Whit-field, Mr. Jimmy Edwards, and Miss Alma Cogan.

"Cinderella" gets her big radio chance

From a London Staff Reporter

"TAKE IT FROM HERE" will have two newcomers in the cast when it returns to the air on November 12. Chosen to fill the big gap left by Joy Nichols—now in Australia—are 21-year-old Alma Cogan and 27-year-old June Whit-field.

TAKE WHAT FROM WHERE?—Radio's "Take It from Here" team are overjoyed at the prospect of doing a broadcast from Bristol on January 16. This picture was taken to show how glad they are. Happily standing are Mr. James Edwards, Miss June Whitfield, Miss Alma Cogan and Mr Richard Bentley. Delightedly seated are Mr Charles Maxwell, the producer; Mr Dennis Norden and Mr Frank Muir, the script-writers; and a microphone. Mr Wallas Eaton was too beside himself with joy to join the group.

s Alma Cogan, singer, has n picked for radio's "Take from Here," which resumes ext month. So has . . .

. . AND JUNE

. . Miss June Whitfield, actress. In the show she and Miss Cogan replace Miss Joy Nichols, now in Australia.

Take It From Here

A highlight of my career was joining the long-running radio show *Take It From Here* – it had been running since 1948 – written by Frank Muir and Denis Norden. Alma Cogan and I took over from Joy Nichols, Alma singing and me talking. My arrival in 1953 coincided with the creation of the dysfunctional family 'the Glums'. Jimmy Edwards as Pa Glum, bombastic and overbearing, his more than dim son Ron – Dick Bentley – and Ron's ever-loving fiancée Eth – me. Mother Glum – a voice from upstairs, shouted at by Pa – was Alma. Wallis Eaton was the fictional pub-owner and any other male voice.

WEEK ENDING JANUARY 15 1955   EVERY WEDNESDAY FOURPENCE

ILLUSTRATED

BBC

Cover girls

Alma Cogan
and
June Whitfield

Picture-profile of two new stars

JUNE WHITFIELD
—ANYONE BUT HERSELF

JUNE WHITFIELD specializes in voices portraying different types of women. Hysterical women are her favourites, but she can make her voice as small and high-pitched as a six-year-old's. And she somehow manages to look the sort of woman she is playing, even when rehearsing in an old skirt and jumper without stage make-up. Her singing voice—she calls it her "golden tones" has never been heard on radio; only twice on television.

June entered R.A.D.A. at the age of seventeen, with the intention of being a straight actress. Two years later she was touring the country with repertory companies. In 1947 she had her only experience of pantomime, as Cinderella to Wilfred Pickles's "Buttons." By the time she came to be in *Love From Judy*, in London, she knew that her real talent was for musical comedy.

Her only two singing records so far are "Seven Lonely Days" and "Diamonds Are A Girl's Best Friend." Her genius for interpreting other types of women means that she seldom gets a chance to be herself.

She once described the part she shares with Alma Cogan in *Take It From Here*. "Alma is the singing half of the partnership," she said. "I just make noises off."

"Oh, Ron...
Yes, Eth?"

"Oh, Ron . . ."

" Yes, Eth ? "

"Something's worrying you, isn't it, beloved ? You've
hardly glanced at your horror-comic."

" Yes, Eth. I am worried. We've had some rather
disturbing news about rich Uncle Charlie."

"What news, Ron ? "

" He's getti[...]

"Poor Ron. Oh,
us a small legacy.
the money ? "

" Count it,

" No, after that, Ron. I think we should invest it. We
must think of what'll happen when we're married."

" I never think of anything else, Eth."

" I mean the extra expense, Ron. Especially if we have
children. And I read an advert. which said that if
you invest in the Co-operative Permanent Building Society,
you get two pound ten a year interest for every hundred."

" But suppose we don't have a hundred children, Eth."

" Try and concentrate, beloved. I'm talking about the
legacy. And as the income-tax on it is paid by the
Society — well, Ron, the 2½% interest we'll get can be
equal to more than 4½%."

" Oh, Eth, I am a lucky Ron Glum to have a fiancée
who understands " per-cents ". My Dad's always saying
he wishes I had a brain like yours. Or anybody's."

" Just the same, Ron, you're the one rich Uncle Charlie
will be leaving the money to. I won't send a postcard
to the Society for more details unless you give the
say-so. What do you think of the idea, Ron ? "

" I like it, Eth."

Written specially for this advertisement by Frank Muir and Denis Norden

LAUGHTER IN THE AIR

FRANKIE HOWERD: "I like
your dress."
Vanessa Lee: "Oh, it's nothing
much."
Frankie Howerd: "That's
what I like about it."
The Frankie Howerd Show.

VIC OLIVER: "It was one of
those high-class joints.
They don't serve ladies at the
bar. You have to bring your
own."
Variety Playhouse.

PETER SELLARS (American):
" I'm over here to find out
how you English live."
Ted Ray: "So, it's got you
worried too, has it?"
Ray's a Laugh.

JUNE WHITFIELD: " You
used to call me your Marilyn
Monroe."
Dick Bentley: "That was be-
fore I saw Marilyn Monroe."
Take It From Here.

BENNY HILL (talks about an
Army friend): " He was in
such bad shape his uniform
fitted."

Bob Monkhous[...]
me if I knew a[...]
kissing. I though[...]
as I was kissing h[...]
Worke[...]

BEBE DANIE[...]
know what[...]
a little dumb cr[...]
at you with a p[...]
Ben Lyon: "[...]
want a new hat[...]
Life [...]

MAX WALL[...]
see me d[...]
I wear out my[...]
inside!"

David Nixo[...]
wasn't long [...]
greatest con[...]
world of mus[...]
juring!"
Henry H[...]

GLADYS [...]
of thos[...]
dyed by her[...]

David Nixon:[...]
us all alike. He has no favourites. He hates everybody."
Midday Music Hall.

133

June Whitfield and Dick Bentley present "Life with the Glums."
"What's it feel like, getting a job for the first time, Ron?" "I don't
like it, Eff!"

Frank and Denis wrote the Glums because they had tired of BBC Radio's
perfect families like the Dales and the Huggets. The Glums started as a
short sketch and soon became half of the show. I loved the writing, their
use of puns and misinterpretation of words, as when Pa said to Eth: 'We've
got to find Ron a job, Eth. Let's have a look in the paper... Here we are,
"Sits Vacant". Well, if that doesn't describe Ron, I don't know what does.'
TIFH took me through seven happy years – sometimes two series a year.

Frank and Denis really started a trend. Nowadays there's hardly a
family portrayed on radio or TV without dysfunctional members – look
at *Eastenders* and they all live in one square.

THE BRITISH BROADCASTING CORPORATION

HEAD OFFICE: BROADCASTING HOUSE, LONDON, W.I

TELEVISION CENTRE: WOOD LANE, LONDON, W.12

TELEPHONE: SHEPHERDS BUSH 8030 ★ TELEGRAMS & CABLES: BROADCASTS, TELEX,

Ref: 35/RW   December, 1954

Dear ~~June Whitfield~~

On Christmas Day we are having once agai
Television Christmas Party to be transmitted fr
7.50 - 9.30 p.m. from Studio "G" at Lime Grove.
will be a real party by the way - the drinks wi
"practical" and not "props"!

We want to invite to this party as many
"Television Family" as possible, whether they b
Writers, Producers, Designers, or what have you
already arranged for about ten or a dozen peop
actually entertain or perform in the party, bu
be very glad if you would care to come along a
on that night, with a partner if you wish, and
the dancing, party games, eating and drinking
merriment.

One has, unfortunately, to bring in the
of money into what should be a happy atmospher
told we can offer you the sum of Three Guinea
transport costs you may have.

If, as I hope, you can come would you
Mr. Bill Lyon-Shaw know at the above address
possible, preferably by telephone. Dress wi
or ladies equivalent and we should like you t
"G" at 6.45 p.m. at the latest so that what l
pre-organisation there will be can be done be
exposed to the startled gaze of the viewing m

Best wishes,

Yours,

(Ronald Waldman)
Head of Television Light Entert

A

25.3.58.

MISS JUNE WHITFIELD

T.I.F.H. 10 YEARS. LUNCH COUNCIL
SIR IAN JACOB.   CHAMBER.

Langham 4468   BROADCASTING HOUSE
Broadcasts Telex London
                                     LONDON W.I

                                     26th February 1958

Dear Miss Whitfield,

I am delighted to hear that you can join us
for the Celebration Luncheon to mark the Tenth
Anniversary of "TAKE IT FROM HERE". It will be
held in the Council Chamber at Broadcasting House
on Tuesday, 25th March, at 12.45 p.m. I look
forward to seeing you then.

Yours sincerely,

Ian Jacob

Director-General

Miss J. Whitfield,
26, Holland Villas Road,
London, W.14.

Charles Maxwell, our producer, kept us in order and the Captain's Cabin, the pub around the corner from our studio (alas no more), 'the Paris' in Lower Regent Street, kept us all in a happy mood.

Radio Times (Incorporating World-Radio) October 16, 1959. Vol. 145: No. 1875.

OCTOBER 18—24

TELEVISION BBC AND SOUND

RADIO TIMES

PRICE FOURPENCE

Jimmy Edwards   Dick Bentley

June Whitfield

IN

'Take It From Here'

What has become of the Glums? Did Ron marry Eth
after all? Did he get across the road to the church?
Or was it only Mr. Glum who saw that open manhole?
Don't miss the first instalment of a new series in the
LIGHT PROGRAMME ON THURSDAY

'BOLD NELSON'S PRAISE'
A PROGRAMME FOR TRAFALGAR DAY

BARON STUDIOS
2 · BRICK STREET
PARK LANE · W · 1
GRO 4441-2-3

Miss June Whitfield,
Saville Theatre,
Shaftesbury Avenue,   22nd January, 1954.
W.C.2.

Dear Miss Whitfield,

    We should very much like the opportunity of
photographing you, as we are extending our library of
theatrical personalities. Naturally, the proofs would
be submitted for your approval before we released any
photographs for publication.

    If you can spare a little time to visit our
Studios, would you be kind enough to contact me so that
a suitable appointment can be made.

        Yours sincerely,

        Margaret Cartier

        Margaret Cartier
        Press Executive.

PHOTO CENTRE LTD.   DIRECTORS: H. R. EYRE, B.

(Above) Left to right: Wallas Eaton, Jimmy Edwards, Dick Bentley and me in Take it from Here. (Left and below left) Being invited to this and that goes with the job.

(Opposite) Note the antique size of an original BBC mike.

The Directors of Associated Newspapers Ltd.
request the pleasure of the company of

Miss June Whitfield, and Guest

at the Presentation of
the National Radio Awards for 1953/4
at the Scala Theatre Charlotte St. W.1.
on Sunday. January 31st. 1954.
to be followed by a Reception

R.S.V.P. to
National Radio Awards,
152 Queen Victoria Street,
London E.C.4.   8.15 p.m. for 8.45 p.m.

BEFORE YOUR VERY EYES

Arthur Askey's new series, with June Whitfield in the cast, ★ starts on Monday at 8.30 p.m.

Arthur Askey

Working with Arthur Askey was a joy – a really funny man. When asked what he was working on, he'd reply, 'Oh, the usual old rubbish.' I joined him in several TV series, beginning with *Before Your Very Eyes* in 1955. He was the first to talk directly to the camera, frowned upon by 'the powers that be', as the camera was supposed to represent the 'fourth wall', as in the theatre.

In one sketch, live of course and black and white, we were in the desert. Halfway through, Arthur beckoned the camera to follow him to the edge of our set and said to the viewers: 'Isn't it funny, playmates, how the desert ends right here?' He was a kind and generous man and even gave us his Cup Final tickets.

Arthur Askey's "playmate" for his new television series is June Whitfield.

The Importance of Oscar

From Here and There was a revue at the Royal Court Theatre. The cast was half American, half British, and for some strange reason I was in the American group. In the picture (right) I am serenading and caressing an Oscar as the most important thing in a girl's life.

I had so many costumes in this revue (including a Wren, opposite) that I had to change under the stage to be ready for the next sketch.

I met Eth—and what a shock I got!

JUNE WHITFIELD is slim, vivacious and blonde and her public fame is based on two words: "Oh, Ron!"

She is known to you as Eth, the eternal fiancee of Ron, the professional moron in radio's most amusing family, the Glums of "Take It From Here."

To June, the Glums have been both a blessing and a curse.

A blessing because the Eth part helped to establish her as a natural comedienne; a curse because radio comedy has obscured her other talents.

Quick-change

Very varied are those other talents, too. June brilliantly proved that when she opened in a new revue, "From Here and There," in London this week.

For two hours, she is rarely off the stage.

With the speed of a quick-change artist, she is seen as a baby in a pram, a grannie, a landlady, a Wren and a debutante being thrown round the stage at her first dancing lesson.

She has one witty, show-stopping number as an ambitious film star.

The sight of her in Monroe-ish blonde wig and spangled sheath of a dress singing a song about preferring a platinum swimming pool to true love should do a lot to kill the curse of the Glums.

Not that she isn't grateful for the chance that "Take It From Here" gave her. "But, she says with a grin, "the part of Eth was not really very satisfying.

"And when my friends kept sidling up to me and saying, ' Oh, Ron,' in a rather ghastly way I began to cringe visibly."

☆ ★ ☆

AT 29, June Whitfield can hope for bigger things. She has an impressive catalogue of experience to offer.

She was trained, impeccably, at RADA (how refreshing to talk to someone who wasn't discovered in a restaurant).

Since then she has been in musicals—"Love From Judy" and "South Pacific"; in repertory; in cabaret ("never again"); and in "Women of Twilight"; (in America it flopped.).

She has even toured in "The Desert Song" and been in pantomime (twice) as Cinderella to Wilfred Pickles'

My Husband

(Opposite) Engagement to
my dear Tim in 1955. We
were married soon after and
shared 45 happy years.

Tim had been in the cricket
First Eleven for his school,
Charterhouse. In the photo
below he is circled, standing
on the right. Other well-
known names in the team
were Peter May, who would
go on to captain England at
cricket, the future Cabinet
minister Jim Prior and the
author Simon Raven.

A cad in the making: Raven in the Charterhouse First XI (sitting extreme right, with James Prior standing third from
the right and subsequent England cricket captain Peter May sitting second from the left) and as a rake about town

Ron's "Eth" To Wed

Oh, Ron . . . you've a rival

Ron Glum's Eth wi marry someone els

Daily Sketch Reporter

JUNE WHITFIELD, Take It From Here star, who plays Eth in a weekly radio courtship with Dick Bentley as Glum, is engaged.

She is to marry Timothy Aitchison, a veyor. He is a broth the Whitfields' family

eternal fiancée of Ron Glum, in radio's "Take It From Here." Yesterday she announced her engagement to 27-year-old Timothy Aitchison, Midhurst, Here they a glistening

NEWS CHRONICLE. 9.8.

Eth's going to wed—TIMs

MISS JUNE WHITFIELD— Eth, the fiancée of Ron in radio's "Take It From Here" — and her real-life fiance, Timothy Aitchison, a 27-year-

old surveyor in Midhurs Sussex. Their engagement wa announced yesterday. Million have followed the courtship Eth and Ron (Dick Bentley

Court, W.8.

RADIO'S ETH TO MARRY

OOOH ETH! WHAT WILL RON SA'

'Fancy jilting him when he's on his hols'

Daily Mirror Reporter

TAKE it from me, Ron Glum (alias Dick Bentley) — YOU'VE BEEN JILTED.

Eth (alias June Whitfield), your fiancee in radio's "Take It From Here" show, is REALLY engaged.

June, the slim comedienne whose "Oooh Ron" became the best-known catch phrase in the show, is to marry a surveyor.

June, 29, was so ex-

Dick Bentley

cited about her real fiance yesterday. In best "Eth-style" she cried "He's G-O-R-G-E-O-U-S!"

A Bit Younger

Then, hastily dropping Eth in favour of June, she said quite primly: "He's tall, dark and

handsome and a little bit younger than me.

HE is Timothy Aitchison of Midhurst, Sussex, a brother of June's doctor. June and Timothy

met at a hotel last Christmas.

June was waiting to go on-stage at the Royal Court Theatre, London, yesterday. She is appearing in "From Here and There" and is

seen in qui ss a baby granny, a Wren and Her fiance see the sh

He is a h watch his

"I shall show busine married.

"When We have It will pro be between and an eve ance of the now.

In Austral

"Take I starts agai and I could could I?"

And what G Australia for the n From here Comedian wards—Ro the radio of the cigs

"It . . thi this telegra DEAR E BELIEVE DO THIS WHEN HE ON HIS REN-HEAR GLUM

"MANCHESTER EVENING NEWS"

DAILY HERALD August 9 1955 5

Oh, Ron . . . you've a rival

Herald Reporter

J

Shoo! for Ron

RON? I've got thing to tell you

You know name is not really Eth. It's June Whitfield. And there's another man in my and now he wants

Well, what Eth? I mean June.

"He's very nice, Ron. You'll like him. His name is Timothy Aitchison and he's a sur—

No Threat From Ron

Tim regularly attended *TIFH*, so at least he knew about the Ron and Eth situation. He was never keen on having his photo taken and probably wondered what on earth he'd taken on. Luckily for me, it didn't put him off. He was soon a friend of my radio fiancé Dick and his wife Peta, and Jimmy too. There was no threat from Ron. As Pa Glum had remarked of Ron and Eth's relationship, 'They're going steady. If they go any steadier, they'll be motionless.'

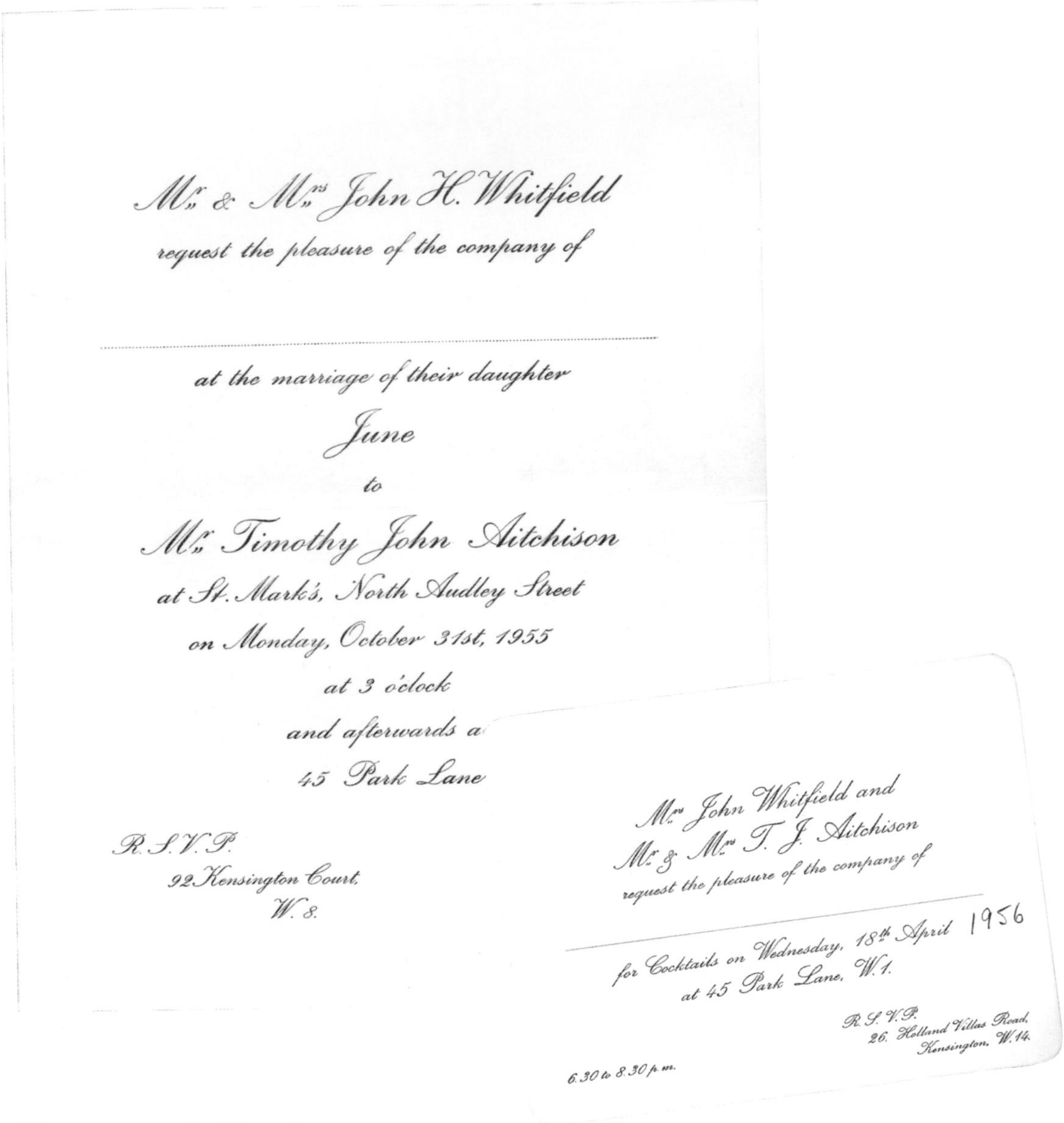

Mr. & Mrs. John H. Whitfield

request the pleasure of the company of

---

at the marriage of their daughter

June

to

Mr. Timothy John Aitchison

at St. Mark's, North Audley Street

on Monday, October 31st, 1955

at 3 o'clock

and afterwards a

45 Park Lane

R.S.V.P.
92 Kensington Court,
W. 8.

Mr. John Whitfield and
Mr. & Mrs. T. J. Aitchison
request the pleasure of the company of

---

for Cocktails on Wednesday, 18th April 1956
at 45 Park Lane, W.1.

R.S.V.P.
26. Holland Villas Road,
Kensington. W.14.

6.30 to 8.30 p.m.

Joy and Sadness

Tim and I were due to marry on 31 October 1955. But my
father had not been well and his condition had worsened,
so we were in no mood for the forthcoming celebration.
We married quietly a week earlier than planned. My dearest
Dad died at Christmas that year. The postponed wedding
celebration was held in April 1956.

Glum outlook for Ron: Eth weds

"Eth," the eternal fiancee of "Ron Glum" in the radio show "Take It From Here," has married.

The announcement said that on Monday "Eth," in real life Miss June Whitfield, actress who has also played in repertory. cabaret, pantomime and musical shows, married Mr. Timothy John Aitchison, a surveyor, of Midhurst (Sussex). Our picture of the bride and bridegroom was taken when their engagement was announced a few months ago.

The bridegroom is the younger son of Commander J. G. Aitchison, R.N., and Mrs. Aitchison, of Ashfield House, Midhurst. Miss Whitfield's home is in Kensington Court, London.

The wedding was to have taken place at St. Mark's, North Audley Street, next Monday afternoon. Instead, Miss Whitfield and Mr. Aitchison became husband and wife last Monday afternoon. About 10 members of the family were present.

The reason for the change of plans was announced by Mrs. John H. Whitfield, June's mother, this afternoon, and is being sent to all the 350 guests. Her husband is critically ill. It was felt that a big stage wedding would be unsuitable, but it is hoped to hold a reception later.

SPOTLIGHT ON—

June Whitfield

She's on TV tonight (Wednesday) in "Fast and Loose"

THE big question that attractive 27-year-old June Whitfield is asking herself is: Where Do I Go From Here? June has made a big success in show business in a very short time—it's only just over two years, in fact, since she got her Big Break in the London musical *Love From Judy*. It kept her busy in the theatre until May this year.

In the meantime she had won a top radio spot in *Take It From Here* and has just signed her contract to appear in it again this winter. She is currently making a big hit in the Bob Monkhouse show *Fast and Loose*.

But June isn't anxious for a life divided between radio and television. She is waiting for that big stage part to come along.

"I'm terrified of television, though I like it very much. It makes a big change from the theatre; appearing night after night in the same thing gets tedious. In television things are changing all the time, but I can't imagine swapping a life of the theatre with a live audience for a battery of cameras and microphones."

A theatre management did send her a play to read—to see if she liked it enough to appear in it. "It was a comedy but I read it from cover to cover and didn't laugh once. I politely declined the offer," she said.

Show business is full of surprises—as June found out. She began her career in conventional fashion: a spell at the Royal Academy of Dramatic Art, a period of acting in repertory and then an assault on the Mecca of London's West End.

She achieved a number of small parts—including one in *South Pacific*—but when it came to the larger rôles theatre managements preferred the names that were known at the box-office.

June thought it was quite a triumph when she secured a part in the cast that was to take the highly successful *Women of Twilight* to New York. A part in a play on Broadway! It sounded good.

It sounded better than it was—the play folded up in seven days.

"While I was out there I met an American song writer who had just written the music to *Love From Judy*. He introduced me to Emile Littler who was over in the States to consider transferring the play to the London stage. He cast me for the second lead."

So after travelling three thousand miles June Whitfield got the break she was waiting for—a leading rôle in the West End!   G.H.G.

Bob Monkhouse

My first TV appearance was in a series of sketches and songs in *The Passing Show* in 1951. My first series was *Fast and Loose* in 1954 with Bob Monkhouse and Denis Goodwin. They wrote the show. Bob was a brilliant actor and comic and later a renowned after-dinner speaker. A great loss to our profession.

Opposite is a formal portrait by Houston Rogers. Ciggies were the thing in the forties and fifties.

The team of Monkhouse, Goodwin, and producer Kenneth Carter was formidably reinforced by June Whitfield, who showed herself as delicious a mimic on vision as she is in "Take It From Here." She should be a permanent fixture if TV can keep her from her destined place as a star of West End revue.

THE UTMOST IN GOONERY

Now you can see madness ...ell as hear it

'Eth' is a Good Trouper

JUNE WHITFIELD is ready to play any part that comes along—which means th... she's just the girl for the new show "T... Idiot Weekly Price 2d." on ITV

AT the age of eight June Whitfield was a Shakespearean actress. Her parents, both amateur players, introduced her to the London suburban Streatham Shakespeare Players and re-joiced at her success in such rôles as Puck in *A Midsummer-Night's Dream.*

Now, twenty-two years later, and a polished professional, Miss Whitfield is still petite, pretty and puckish but definitely not Shakespearean. Her voice, with which she won a prize at the Royal Academy of Dramatic Art, is best-known as a nasal whine in radio's *Take It From Here.* She is Ron Glum's eternally affianced Eth.

But she can voice more than her plaintive catch-phrase "Oh, Ron!" As ITV viewers have found to their delight, the Whitfield girl can sing. This will come as no surprise to West End theatre-goers who can remember her taking over two years ago from Jean Carson in the musical *Love From Judy.*

Though she trained as a straight actress at RADA and had singing lessons when she was 17, her sense of humour is now being given slightly more scope in Show Business than any of her other attributes.

Yet a dossier on June Whitfield would list diverse public appearances. Her RADA lessons were put to the test in *Appointment With Fear,* and *The Cure For Love* with Wilfred Pickles. There followed panto with Pickles and her first West End appearance in the Coward show *Ace of Clubs.*

She was then to be seen in the revue *Penny Plain* and the musical *South Pacific.* Back to the legitimate theatre with *Women Of Twilight* which took her to New York; but not for long.

Darkness fell after onl... Last year in the London... *Here And There* Miss Wh... happier experience. She... astic notices from the cri...

The dossier must also... *Nursing* (BBC), Devon... baby noises. "I am qui... and take what's dished... Whitfield, the good tro...

Having appeared wi... house on TV she is w... *The Idiot Weekly Pri...* Peter Sellers show, in... see her this week.

The Whitfield recip... artist's TV tummy i... camera is a very de... on..."

Unlike the unfortunate Eth (she has played the part for more than two years), she is now happily married. Her husband is Timothy Aitchison, a surveyor—and she detected a momen-tary gleam in his eye when she revealed that before RADA she learned short-hand and typing.

She watches her husband play hockey in winter and cricket in sum-mer. This is pleasant, she finds—for she has never had a hobby. Though it is not true that—as one writer has said of her—"June grew up with greasepaint on her mind if not on her features."

"I never had a burning desire to go on the stage," says Miss Whitfield. "But it was always made easy for me —nobody tried to stop me."

What of the future? She isn't worrying. "I'm rather enjoying being married at the moment," she told me. And she sounded far from Glum.

J. P. G.

ITA viewers looking for a short cut to insanity are recommended to "The Idiot Weekly" on Friday. Here is the editorial staff having their chips—(from the left) June Whitfield, Max Geldray, Patti Lewis, Peter Sellers, Kenneth Connor and Graham Stark

'This is crazier,' says 'Eth' ▶

by JACK BELL

COMEDIAN Peter Sellers winds up his "Yes, It's the Cathode Ray Tube Show" series on ITV at 9.30 tonight.

He is to make a film in which he will play FIVE different parts.

Appearing tonight with Peter and the other "Cathode Ray" stal-warts, Michael Bentine and David Nettheim, is June Whitfield—"Eth" from radio's "Take It From Here" show.

Comments June: "I thought our 'TIFH' re-hearsals were crazy. But they're nothing compared with 'YITCRTS'!"

21

June Whitfield discovers what happens to young ladies who take the mickey out of commercial TV. Man with the cosh is Sellers

Yes, It's the Cathode Ray Tube Show

Yes, It's the Cathode Ray Tube Show followed three series known as *The Freds*, written by Spike Milligan, who handed over to Michael Bentine for *YITCRTS*. Quite mad and definitely Goon-ish. Peter Sellers was a chameleon. You never quite knew on any day which colour he would be.

Hancock, the great radio comic, moves over to TV

By THOMAS E. BERGMAN

TONY HANCOCK, who is possibly the greatest radio comedian since Tommy Handley, is to be seen in his new television show next Monday. ~~2301~~

Hancock's Half-Hour will consist of six fortnightly shows and will be written by the same scriptwriters who provide Hancock's radio material. Sidney James, busy filming, will be out of the casts for the first two performances. With Hancock will be Richard Wattis. June Whitfield and Kenneth Williams.

JUNE WHITFIELD

~~2301~~

June Is Versatile

IT is going to seem rather odd to see JUNE WHITFIELD, who has a big part in the current TONY HANCOCK series, without hearing her utter the expected words . . . "Oh, Ron."

Those words helped June to fame when she and Alma Cogan took over from Joy Nichols in radio's famous "Take It From Here." June played "Eth" to Dick Bentley's "Ron." And "Eth" helped build June into a top liner.

That's not her only experience of taking over. She also hit the headlines when, from a small part in the stage hit "Love From Judy," she was hurtled into the lead when Jean Carson went sick.

Friday

But there's nothing of the "takeover" about her in to-night's show. She has been deliberately chosen; because of her fine sense of fun and comedy; her personality; and her voice.

Yes, June is another Whitfield who sings. Not surprising really. She once sang in pantomime with . . . you'll never guess who . . . Wilfred Pickles! 8.30 p.m.

THE BRITISH BROADCASTING CORPORATION

HEAD OFFICE: BROADCASTING HOUSE, LONDON, W.I

TELEVISION CENTRE: WOOD LANE, LONDON, W.12

TELEGRAMS & CABLES: BROADCASTS, LONDON, TELEX * INTERNATIONAL TELEX 2-2182

TELEPHONE: SHEPHERDS BUSH 8030

18th March 1957

Dear Miss Whitfield,

I enclose script of "Hancock's Half Hour" (1) for transmission on Monday, 1st April, 1957, in which you have kindly agreed to play the part of Miss Duboir.

Your rehearsal dates are 25th, 26th, 27th March at the Inns of Court Mission, 46 Drury Lane, and 30th March in Rm.2, Canteen Block, Television Centre.

Mr. Wood looks forward to seeing you at 10.30am on Monday, 25th March.

Yours sincerely,

S. Adams

(for Duncan Wood)

Miss June Whitfield,
26 Holland Villas Road,
London, W.14.

He's ROUGH
MARLON HANCOCK steels himself . . . while June Whitfield steals a little affection

. . . and dangerous to know
MARSHAL HANCOCK . . . "Are you a Matt or a mouse?" asks June

Tony Hancock

Tony Hancock's first TV show *Hancock's Half Hour*. Here we are sending up well-known film characters such as (top) Marlon Brando and Vivien Leigh in *Streetcar Named Desire*.

The letter opposite is a good example of the BBC's impeccable manners and formal approach of the time.

The Blood Donor

The photo from this famous episode of the 1961 series *Hancock* by Alan Simpson and Ray Galton has Tony, the nervous and reluctant blood donor, me as the nurse and in the middle, Frank Thornton, waiting to give blood. All of us taking part knew it was a very funny script, but we had no idea it would prove to be immortal. It was difficult to stifle laughter when Tony was walking around the waiting room singing the poster headlines – 'Drink A Pint of Milk A Day' and 'Coughs and Sneezes Spread Diseases' – to the tune of 'Deutschland Über Alles'.

Alan and Ray reproduced the show for radio in 2009, with the same story but different characters. My daughter Suzy played the nurse. Time marches on...

(Opposite top) me as a seductress in Tony's first TV series and below, ten years later in Tony's final series for British television, dressed as a bunny girl, Esmeralda Staveley-Smythe, in a nightclub sketch.

CHARMING: With June Whitfield during the recording of his TV show in 1967

ETH takes it from there

TV by Kenneth Baily

June Whitfield—there's a race to make her a big star of TV

ONE of the advantages the B.B.C. has gained over commercial TV is that pretty, clever Miss who signs her name June Whitfield—and is known to radio's " Take It From Here " listeners as " Eth."

For June, a radio star of two years' standing, is now becoming a B.B.C. television topliner largely because rival TV started raiding the radio star stables.

When Lime Grove tied many of its TV personalities to contracts barring them from commercial, the plug-TV chiefs began luring the big names of radio over to their camp.

So Lime Grove put June into the Bob Monkhouse shows and she appeared there before her first commercial TV date came along. June is still free to appear on both networks.

In fact, life is full for the twenty-seven year old Yorkshire lass who has blithely stepped into other stars' shoes. June followed Joy Nichols in " Take It From Here "—having previously appeared with Joy's husband, Wally Peterson, in " South Pacific."

Then, when Jean Carson fell out of the big musical, " Love From Judy," it was June who took her sta[...]

But on t[...] network TV [...] June is nov[...] as a " your[...] June mea[...]

career for the time being. And, as far as I can see, her next lap will be a race between B.B.C. and CTV to make her a big TV star.

AT THE MOMENT LIME GROVE IS JUST ABOUT LEADING BY A COUPLE OF PROGRAMMES. . . .

"Pops" Tops

THIS is a peak season for the " pop " singers. Now that the B.B.C. has " Hit Parade," as well as " Off The Record," the best - selling vocalists are streaming into Lime Grove week by week.

And, every Saturday afternoon, CTV has its " Music Shop " promotion of the recording stars. Who are the boys and girls who are coming [...] these TV song

record shows, considers Dennis Lotis a fine acquisition.

But Brighton's ex-lifeguard Tony Reid is justifying both TV networks' bookings of him by bringing in the most mail. Tony is a swimming champion and former boxer.

On the girls' side Betty Miller, already established, is being promoted TV-wise whenever she is free to take the dates.

But two newcomers are on the Lime Grove " build-up " line. A recent arrival from Scotland, twenty-six year old Annie Ross, made a big impression on CTV.

Then young Pauline Shepherd has already clocked up three CTV shows, following her discovery at Lime Grove.

Price Of Secrecy

Grove probe fell on Ted Ray, some of the most amusing and moving aspects of his life never came out.

So long as the subjects chosen for the show do not know beforehand, the B.B.C. cannot include in the script material that the star alone can provide.

When Ted Ray met his sisters, the encounter reminded him of a number of incidents. But other visitors from his [...] called for by the [...]

Radio and Television Programmes

A Carefree New Series For Comedian Ted Ray

DAPPER comedian Ted Ray returns to the air tonight with June Whitfield in a show called The Spice of Life, a carefree mixture of comedy and music (West and Home 8.15).

Featured with him are Deryck Guyler, Gene Crowley, Therese Burton, " Hutch," as the voice of romance, Sid Phillips, and the Coronets.

JUNE WHITFIELD who appears in the new Ted Ray show (West, 8.50).

The Spice of Life

Ted, Ray and I were Mrs Pinny and Mrs Drool, a couple of ladies in a launderette, for a sketch in Ted's radio show each week. I also popped up as various debs, tarts and old bats, according to the script. I also joined Ted in a couple of episodes of his TV show, *It's Saturday Night*. What a funny, witty man he was and a pleasure to work with.

The Straker Special

This was a TV musical comedy with Denis Quilley, in which I played a tomboy mechanic and Denis the factory owner's son. It nearly didn't happen. I woke up one day with a nasty pain, which turned out to be appendicitis. We had started rehearsals, but I was rushed off to hospital. Associated Rediffusion kindly postponed the dates of the show and it was recorded when I had recovered from my emergency operation.

9.0   **Time signal**

THE STRAKER SPECIAL
A new television musical
starring

JUNE WHITFIELD   and   **DENIS QUILLEY**

Book by Donald Monat and
June Dixon
Lyrics by Donald Monat
Music by Basil Tait
with
Adrienne Corri
Laurie Payne
Sam Kydd
Cyril Ornadel and his Orchestra
Musical numbers staged by Tommy Linden
Settings by Timothy O'Brien
Produced and directed by
Kenneth Carter

1956

28   TV TIMES   November 16, 1956

SPANNER IN THE WORKS

THE scene is the London flat of an attractive actress. It is mid-morning. The actress, and a young man, are seated cosily on a settee [befor]e a warm electric fire. They are completely [alone] in the flat.

[Hi]s voice is husky as he talks to her, almost in a [whisp]er. (He has a cold.)

[He]r piercing blue eyes are misty. (He has blown [cigar]ette smoke into them.)

[Th]ey speak. Of romance? No—of internal com[bust]ion engines.

[This] is not such a surprising subject. The actress is [June] Whitfield. She is to play the female lead in *The [Stra]ker Special* on Thursday. The title role is played [by a] £2,000 racing car. June's part is that of an expert [mec]hanic.

[And] he looks at me (I'm the young man) and says softly: [Le]t's not talk of exhaust [ma]nifolds and high com[pre]ssion ratios."

As I couldn't care less [ab]out same—unless I gave the matter my [mo]st serious consideration—I agree.

Says June: "In fact we can't talk about [th]em. I don't know one end of a motor-[ca]r from another."

Considering she's supposed to know [m]ore than one end of a spanner from the [ot]her in this musical comedy—written [spe]cially for ITV and for June—this was [in]teresting. How, then, was she to give the [im]pression she knew what it was all about?

June explains: "I am told that the [pr]inciple of the 'Straker Special' and my [o]wn baby car is exactly the same . . . [t]hey both have an engine and four wheels [a]nd can be driven.

"What with everything being madly [st]reamlined and weight minimums and [p]ower maximums, and other things I don't [u]nderstand, I'm completely baffled."

"So how do you appear efficient?"

WITH THE STRAKER SPECIALIST

"Oh, it's a simple formula . . . I just do what I'm told."

Ever had the feeling that two eyes are burning holes in your back? I got it right about this time. Sitting on a chair, tucked away in a corner of a room, was Mr. Bear.

An extremely large teddy bear is this character. So large that either June is two teddies high, or teddy is half a Whitfield high. Take your choice.

"He's my friend," says June. "We grew up together. Only he started smoking young."

At which point we left the flat. June had to go shopping. The bear came with us. He's that kind of a friend.

The car wouldn't start. A wonderful opportunity to see just how good a mechanic Miss Whitfield really was.

"What do you usually do when the engine won't start?" I ask, in my best driving-examiner's voice.

"Look for a phone," says June. "So that I can call the A.A."

"Wouldn't you even lift up the bonnet and look at the engine?"

"There *is* an engine?"

Gag over, she decides to look at the engine. The Straker Special's expert mechanic can't lift the bonnet.

She used to know how it opened, she explained, but now she's forgotten how to lift the catch. Oh, well, to the phone . . .

There is no need. She remembers something she ought to have remembered first time round. When starting a motor car it is always advisable to switch on the ignition first.

We drive to the butcher's. My opinion of women drivers rises. Until she parks about 3 ft. from the pavement. No expert mechanic would do such a thing. Then I discover a small dog eating his dinner in the kerb.

"I'll shift him," says June, holding Mr. Bear out of the window and barking like a dog.

By the time we arrive back at the flat I discover that June has no sense of direction (except on the stage); that she can't memorise travel instructions (but can learn pages of scripts); and that she can't remember names.

"I remember yours, though," she says. I perk up.

"As soon as we arranged this meeting I connected your name with something—it's the only way I ever remember them. When you put the phone down I thought: 'Remember he's connected with a tree' . . . that's how I remembered you were Eric Tree . . . no? Er, Eric Wood? Oh dear, I seem to have forgotten it again."

That she might forget. But one thing she will never forget is *The Straker Special*—she has a scar to remind her about it.

The musical was due to be shown last August 30. Filmed excerpts were shot. Rehearsals had been going on for four days. On the night of August 23, June complained of a "tweak in the tummy." A few hours later she was in hospital having her appendix whipped out. The show had to be put off until now.

Eric Linden

A spanner is a girl's best friend . . . Denis Quilley cowers as June Whitfield moves in to the attack — a scene as they will appear in "The Straker Special"

Denis Quilley and June Whitfield star in the new musical, "The Special Day," to be produced and directed by Kenneth Carter on August 30. June plays the part of a garage mechanic and Denis the composer-son of a car manufacturer

So simple really, when you're an expert . . . or a Straker Specialist, rather

AUSTRALIAN Alan White waved to June Whitfield as she walked across the road. June and Alan hadn't met before —but that didn't matter, since their TV sets had already introduced them.

We went into a St Marylebone bar and talked about their new TV series. It is the fortnightly, hour-long, Jack Hylton production, *On With the Show,* which starts next Thursday.

A few months ago, Alan was in the Saturday serial *McCreary Moves In.* Now he is moving on—to the role of comedy actor.

Alan and June had both run through the first script of their new programme, and were pleased about what it offered. Said June: "We're not cast as husband and wife —except perhaps in individual sketches—because the series will be based on different comedy situations. We will range from a courting couple to a businessman and his secretary."

Said Alan: "Between glossy production numbers and spots by guest singers we shall be trying to get laughs—not from gags but from the kind of predicaments we all find ourselves in."

June said: "The new series offers scope for new characters —and I like playing characters so much."

When Alan came to England from Sydney three years ago, he brought an open-air look from "down under." "But I don't miss those sun-scorched beaches—you'd be surprised how after 30 years you can feel you've had too much sun. Since arriving here I've only had one holiday—a few days in Paris."

His 12 years in Australian repertory and radio was followed by more theatre work and films in England—including a stage version of *Doctor in the House* which ran eight months. "The 'McCreary' serial gave me a liking for TV, and I feel this new comedy series is a really good break."

His ambition? Said 33-year-old Alan: "I've been an actor 15 years—but I still think it's too early to say what my ambition

IT'S ON WITH THE SHOW —FOR LAUGHS

It's fun getting there on a bicycle built for one

is. I'm ready to let those who know more about these things tell me what I can do best. So I'm pleased with the variety of material *On With the Show* offers. I don't think an actor knows what he can do best till he's maybe 45."

The range of characters played by June will mean constant changes. "I have to wear all sorts of dresses. Some my own; some from the wardrobe department. I prefer dresses to suits. For my size, I think they do more. Necklines? I like the boat-line best. I'm not keen on dipping necklines. One thing I like for TV is high shoes. Heels add to my height. Away from the studios, I prefer flat shoes."

"Shoes are an im

too," said Alan. "They are part of actor's make-up. If you have a mysteri part, soft shoes build up a stealthy to Hard-soled shoes do the opposite. Ana TV the noise shoes make—or the lack —is important. It would sound shockin you stamped your way across a p marble floor."

The first programme will be introd by Sidney James, and Welsh baritone Emanuel will be a guest—a pointer t variety the series offers.

During the series, June and her hus will be decorating the house they hav bought in Kensington.

'Oh! Eth' starts her own ITV show

By Philip Phillips

ETH begins her most ambitious TV series tonight.

Who is Eth? She is Britain's most famous, even if somewhat ghastly, sweetheart — Eth, of "Take It From Here's" Ron and Eth.

She is really actress June Whitfield, an attractive, 32-year-old blonde.

And on ITV tonight June stars in the first of a new series called "On With The Show." She will do sketches with actor Alan White.

Also in the cast are Tony Hancock's old foil, Sidney James, comedian Harry Fowler and the Welsh tenor, Ivor Emanuel.

June ha- TV before but, ed to me last t From Here" make her take

On With the Show

Alan White and I were not Syd Ceasar and Imogen Coker, well-known American comics. The scripts were from their American show and had been adapted for us. But their quick-fire repartee didn't really translate and our version of this TV show was not a success. So, on with the next...

(Above) I bought this mink 'tie' and used it to enhance a dress. I loved it. In the 1950s everyone wore fur. It is now carefully packed away. Will it ever be p.c. again?

WET FOR JUNE

"THE rain it raineth every day," but not on All Hallows Fete. For six years that has been true, but on the seventh the rains came and they persisted all day. Yet the crowds still arrived and seemed in no hurry to go home. There were great trees to shelter them and the marquees at least kept the stall-holders and their goods from being washed away. The Army Cadet Force Band made a brave show at the start till Miss JUNE WHITFIELD arrived in a handsome Rolls Royce and accompanied by the Vicar, who first introduced the charming visitor to her hostess, Miss Beatrice Rowla the friendly shelter of the verandah of Croyland Hall. For a few m the lake "Eth" struggled to send her wet balloon into the air and ga the day success, in spite of the elements. She then made a tour of the sideshows, under the shelter of the Vicar's large coloured umbrella stall some purchase was made and most of the sideshows were vi arrow or two at the archery, a shot with a rifle, a throw at the crock an attempt to drown Fr. Osborne, whose umbrella failed to prevent from the over-full bucket above his head. After a rest indoors, the i June made yet another tour of the grounds and did not leave for hor were almost over. Under the great cedar tree, with her husband and great-aunt, she judged the fancy dresses, besides signing autographs and having her picture taken. She even tried to send up another balloon, but the rain still kept it earthbound : only our spirits soared to find so many people still buying hard at the stalls and, although the dancing displays had to be abandoned, the archery club gave a brief display and at six, instead of seven, the Vicar announced the lucky prize-winners, who included himself and his junior

JUNE WHITFIELD TO OPEN FETE

June Whitfield, star of the B.B.C. show "Take It From Here," will open Wellingborough All Hallows Church fete on June 16. She is a

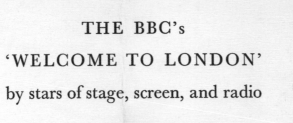

Opening a Fête

Auntie B had moved to Wellingborough, where Uncle Billy had continued as a doctor. She invited me to open the local fête – mission accomplished, in the rain of course. Uncle Billy had died by this time, but it was good to see Auntie B again. She was a great character, she taught me to play bezique and her visiting Irish friend gave me a wonderful 'voice' to use for future radio roles.

Chapter Five

A NEW ADDITION TO THE FAMILY

GENTLY BENTLEY
RON CAN'T BE GLUM WITH ETH'S BABY

"Ron Glum" — Dick Bentley when he's not on the air—called on his old friend "Eth" from the radio show "Take It From Here" yesterday. This was a moment when Bentley had to take gently—the "it" being four-month-old Susan Jane, as "Eth"—June Whitfield—handed her to him in her West London home. Susan is the daughter of June Whitfield and her husband Timothy Aitchison. And yesterday, being Susan's christening day, was a day when "Ron Glum" was at his gayest.

ETH'S BABY GREETS THE CAMERAMAN WITH A YAWN FROM MOTHER'S ARMS

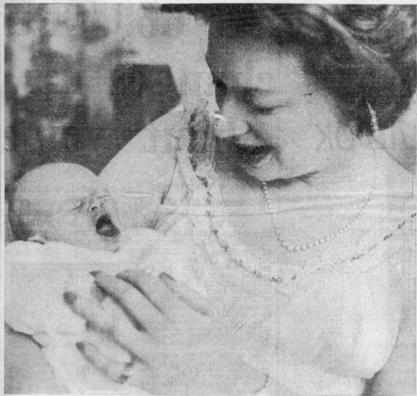

Three-day-old Susan Jane greets the cameraman with a yawn from the arms of mother, actress June Whitfield, at a Welbeck Street maternity hospital today. Miss Whitfield—Eth of radio's Take It From Here show—is married to surveyor Mr. Timothy Aitchison. Susan is their first child.

Baby expecte

June Whitfield—"Eth" radio show Take It From is expecting a baby in three weeks.

And nobody knew abo until today, when Dick —her "Ron"—broke the Adelaide

She is married to Mr. T Aitchison, an ...... su They live in Bayswater. It first baby.

The New Arrival

Our darling daughter Suzy. Good as gold and twice as precious. My greatest achievement – with a little help from her Dad – Tim, not Ron, even if Ron (opposite above) does look proud and besotted.

(Above) Daddy's first glimpse of his tiny daughter.

Suzy

(Above left) Suzy's first boyfriend – I love this snap. (Above right) watching me on TV she said: 'Then Mummy comes home to Suzy'. (Opposite top) A magazine ad with mother and daughter in matching coats. (Opposite bottom) Mother, Tim, me and Suzy – it's Christmas!

1962

14

SUSIE'S COAT IS . . .

JUST LIKE MUMMY'S!

❋

Comedienne June Whitfield loves her cosy, full-length knitted coat, with its air of elegance. And two-year-old Susie is so excited to have a coat just like mummy's. Both coats are knitted in simple rib.

Radio Times (Incorporating World-Radio) November 9, 1961. Vol. 153: No. 1983.

NOVEMBER 11—17

BBC RadioTimes

tv and SOUND

5D

The Seven Faces of Jim
THURSDAY TELEVISION

Jimmy Edwards

(Above) Jimmy's *This is Your Life* in 1958.

Working with Jimmy in *Take It From Here* for seven years, plus three series of *Faces of Jim* and *The Fossett Saga*, we got to know him pretty well. He was the same off-stage as he was on. Jim undoubtedly enjoyed a drink. He used to say, 'I don't drink normally – I drink abnormally.' When he wrote about his time in the Air Force during the war, he headed one chapter, 'Drink Canada Dry – I did my best' (Canada Dry was a well-known ginger ale). He was a larger-than-life character.

Arthur Askey

Arthur's Treasured Volumes
were produced in 1960 by ATV and written by Dave
Freeman – a different volume each week – all fictitious.
Arthur's daughter Anthea, so like her father, started each
episode by taking a book from a shelf and beginning to
read it to her father. The story then came to life with the
rest of the cast. Arthur was as usual completely at home,
ad-libbing as the spirit moved him.

The Faces of Jim (and June)

The Faces of Jim with Jimmy Edwards, Richard Briers and Ronnie Barker, written by Frank Muir and Denis Norden. Great fun and lots of dressing up.

(Opposite, far left corner) Jim, as a Victorian industrialist with an unhappy wife, said: 'Perhaps it would have been better if we'd had a child.' His wife (me), more frustrated than ever, replied: 'We've got a child.'

(Above) Ronnie Barker as Lascivius, a lovelorn Roman officer. I was a Saxon leader and Jimmy (opposite, second down) was the Emperor Hadrian.

More Faces of Jim and Legs of June

We all played so many roles. In this montage opposite, I go from an elderly violinist and an army officer (pipe-smoking, male) to Madam Soo, an oriental lady, and a Russian spy.

CROWTHER'S CROWD

**HOME
1.10**

'Two's company, three's a crowd' —and what a crowd when it's Crowther's. By the end of half-an-hour it will have seemed like a milling throng, yet all the talking, all the impersonations, will have been done by three artists only—**Leslie Crowther, June Whitfield,** and **Ronnie Barker.** Recognise the team? They are the same tightly-knit trio whose regular comedy spots shivered the timbers of Vic Oliver's *Variety Playhouse.* Starting their first fully-fledged series today, Crowther and Company are three students out to reform the world—Leslie the medical student, June the drama student, and Ronnie a trainee at a school for chefs. Thanks to the miracle of radio, listeners can join their summit conferences at El Aroma coffee bar in Bloomsbury. When they can get a note in edgeways, **Mickie Most and the Minute Men** lace the arguments with coffee bar rhythms.

'They'll argue about anything and illustrate their points with impersonations,' said the producer,
~~Johnston.~~ 'There'll
~~After all,~~
~~of mud and~~
~~a programme~~
~~chance to ex-~~
~~with eight or~~
~~on a particu-~~
~~st, on Enter-~~
~~strips off~~
~~ing from disc~~
~~us.'

~~slie Crowther~~
~~idea—letting~~
~~for a whole~~
~~we'll "keep it~~
~~producer's in-~~
structions. June and Ronnie and I must be the closest-knit team in show business. As for our conferences with the script-writers, George Evans and Derek Collyer, they're a riot. We meet in each other's houses and then carry on in the nearest local over darts. If our arguments on the air sound true to life, that's why.'

ERNEST THOMSON

Leslie Crowther

June Whitfield

Ronnie Barker

BBC RADIO

COMPLIMENTARY TICKET NOT FOR SALE ADMIT TWO

The Paris
Regent Street
London S.W.1
(near Piccadilly Circus)

THE PARIS
REGENT STREET, LONDON, S.W.I
[NEAR PICCADILLY CIRCUS]

SOUND
BBC
SOUND

Crowther's Crowd

WITH LESLIE CROWTHER, JUNE WHITFIELD, RONNIE BARKER, AND MICKIE MOST AND THE MINUTE MEN

FRIDAY, 6th DECEMBER
DOORS OPEN 12.40 P.M.
NO ADMITTANCE AFTER 12.55 P.M.

COMPLIMENTARY TICKET
NOT FOR SALE—ADMIT 2

Leslie Crowther

Leslie Crowther, Ronnie Barker and I provided sketches in
Vic Oliver's *Variety Playhouse*, which was mainly music. In 1963
after three series we were given our own radio show, *Crowther's
Crowd*, again written by George Evans and Derek Collyer. It was
an extremely happy association and we enjoyed some great times
in each other's company. Leslie and Tim shared a passion for antique
porcelain – Leslie had a great collection – and we enjoyed visiting
antique markets together. Ronnie was also a collector, especially
of old postcards.

A Steptoe riper than any cuss word

THE Steptoe quarters, a cross between a jackdaw's hideout and a drained duckpond, took on their crummiest look last night when Dad went up West.

Five days of washing up and a litter of opened tins made this familiar set seem like a compost heap.

"The Bonds That Bind Us" was one of the richest of the current B B C episodes of "Steptoe and Son," with Harry H. Corbett at his peak as

LAST NIGHT'S TV
BY RICHARD SEAR

the frustrated 'Arold. His expressions were more vivid than the ripest cuss word.

The plot made him act with all the cunning of Dad — like father, like

son—and emphasised the underlying genius writers Simpson and Galton have built into this series.

Dad's sudden wealth from a Premium Bond win started a perfectly natural reaction—new suit, new choppers and a blonde.

His return with the blonde brought one of those scenes which is the strength of Steptoe — a desperate battle by 'Arold to keep Dad out

of the clutches of a female.

June Whitfield, as the Soho pick-up, was excellent and had some marvellously funny lines.

As is common to the series now, the violins moved in to put an edge on the tears of laughter as Dad realised he was just another ripe pigeon . . . moved in to give the comedy a final lustre unequalled in British television.

OFF-BEAT

FULL MARKS . . . 6508
● TO June Whitfield, for a knife-edged cameo in "Steptoe and Son." The Premium Bond win took the programme too near farce, but

Steptoe and Son

(Opposite) An episode from *Steptoe and Son* – the hugely successful sitcom by Alan Simpson and Ray Galton about two rag-and-bone men. The old boy (Wilfrid Brambell) had won a premium bond, went 'up West' and picked up a girl in Soho (me). We confronted Harold (Harry Corbett, opposite) and I told him I was about to become his 'new mummy'.

BAXTER ON TRAVEL

For the first programme in a new comedy series
Stanley Baxter is joined by June Whitfield

📺
8.0

WE live in an age of the specialist—
the man with microscopic knowledge
of a single subject. **Stanley Baxter**,
however, in his new fortnightly series,
alternating with Jimmy Edwards's
Bold as Brass, shows us that he is a master of
six subjects: travel, television, law, theatre,
class, and films. And tonight it is *Baxter on
Travel*. **June Whitfield** and Stanley (working
together for the first time) have been filming
short comedy sequences with producer **Michael
Mills**, dashing about from Westminster to
Liverpool (where Elizabeth Taylor, bearing an
unearthly resemblance to Mr. Baxter, will be
taking us on a tour of Merseyland), and
squelching about on the mudflats of Southend.
And June will turn her attention to foreign
travel and property that can be rented abroad.

Travel, says the old adage, broadens the
mind, but when the travellers are Stanley
Baxter and June Whitfield you will be happy
that you are settled comfortably at home.

Stanley told us that this series has little in
common with last summer's *The Stanley
Baxter Show*, in that it is not a television
revue. He is simply taking a jaundiced-eye-
view of topics of national interest. In the
series viewers can expect to see some of the
familiar Baxter creations. ' The elderly crusty
character will be turning up again,' he said,
' plus a lot of new ones—and one in particular: S   himself to link
the co
has ar
own
charac

Stanley Baxter
2, Bewdley Street
Islington
N.1.
22 VI '64.

My Dear June,
Here's another big hug
for all your fabulous work on the
show.
I'll keep nagging them till we're
teamed together again on a new series.
Love to that lovely Susie
and kindest regards to Tim.
Viva the Car Hire!
Lots of love,
Stanley
(xxxx)

Baxter and Howerd

I worked with Frankie Howerd on
both TV and radio in the 1960s.
He wasn't so keen on radio. He felt that reading the
script restricted his rapport with the audience in the
studio. In the little picture above right, the exchange
was as follows:

    Me: 'Kiss me, kiss me, bite me... bite me.'
    Frankie: 'Bite you? I'm a vegetarian. Let go of me.'
    (Opposite) With Stanley Baxter in 1964 in his series
'Baxter On...'. I would have loved to do another series
with him – see his letter – well, it's never too late!

On the trail—
of fun!

IN the ceaseless struggle against crime and injustice, there will always be men like "Porterhouse—Private Eye." Bungling, stupid and inefficient. And women like Porterhouse's daughter (Daffodil). Together, they can make a hash of the simplest...

9.10 Six of the Best

See page 7

PRESENTS
Porterhouse—Private Eye
BY MAURICE WILTSHIRE
STARRING
PETER BUTTERWORTH
AND
JUNE WHITFIELD
WITH
DUDLEY FOSTER

CAST
Edwin
  Porterhouse .... Peter Butterworth
Daffodil .... June Whitfield
Otto Mulchrone ...... Dudley Foster
Sir Gregory Bowles . John Glyn Jones
Lady Bowles .... Cicely Hullett
Hargreaves .... Bryan Mosley
Irma .... Elizabeth Counsell
Inspector .... Frank Sieman

DESIGNER RAY WHITE
DIRECTED BY ALBERT LOCKE
PRODUCED BY ALAN TARRANT

Still in Private Four Eyes

Still in the wigs and glasses, always happier in disguise. In *Porterhouse – Private Eye*, I was the inept judo-loving daughter of an equally inept detective played by Peter Butterworth. I worked with Peter in several 'Carry On...' films and in the 'Scott On...' series.

The Spy With a Cold Nose

Another takeover role, this time from Dora Bryan,
who was suffering from a sore throat and advised
to rest. *The Spy With a Cold Nose* had a starry cast.
From the left in the photo: Lionel Jeffries, Laurence
Harvey, me, Eric Sykes. Very exciting – a proper film!

WED JUNE 15, 1966

June takes over Dora's film part

June Whitfield—"Eth" in the
radio series Take It From Here
—was getting her child ready for
school today when the phone
rang.

But she is glad she stopped a
moment to answer it. For she
was offered a big film part.

June is stepping into Dora
Bryan's role in The Spy With A
Cold Nose.

Dora quit

June was taken to the
costumiers from her home in
Wimbledon and she starts filming tomorrow morning.

Dora quit the part because of
a sore throat and she has been
advised not to take on more
work.

The part in the film—it stars
Laurence Harvey, Daliah Lavi
and Eric Sykes—was specially
written for Dora, star of the
West End's hit musical, Hello
Dolly.

Pickles, too

How does June feel about
working with Laurence Harvey?
"I have never met him," she
said, "but I think it is going to
be terrifying working alongside

BBC tv
LIGHT ENTERTAINMENT
presents
COMEDY PLAYHOUSE
'BEGGAR MY NEIGHBOUR'
with
JUNE WHITFIELD
and
PETER JONES

TV

By VIRGINIA IRONSIDE

AS AN IDEA the BBC's
new comedy programme
Beggar My Neighbour is a
winner.

The Garveys and the Butts
are neighbours in the suburbs.
Mr. Garvey is an ill-paid executive; Mr. Butt is an immensely
prosperous factory worker.

The Garveys spend their
time trying to keep up with the
Butts and the Butts spend their
time giggling at the Garveys
trying to keep up with them.

The result should be a
poignant and pungent comment
[on] the materialistic values of
[tod]ay. Or something. Instead
[it's] not accurate enough to be
[sha]rp, yet it's real enough to be
[as b]oring as the situation must
[be i]n real life.

[A]nd probably the saddest part
[of it] is the complete waste of
[June] Whitfield who, I am sure,
[coul]d be an English Lucille Ball.
[She's] pretty, with a lovely clown
[face,] the sort of person who can
[make] a fool of herself and still
[look att]ractive.

[Her]e she is wasted on a script
[that] if it were on the radio
[would]n't be worth listening to
[as a] background to darning

BEGGAR YOUR NEIGHBOUR

and let battle commence in a new comedy series

1
7.30

WHEN you have friends and neighbours,
Bud Flanagan used to assure us, the world
is a happier place. But when the people
next door also happen to be relatives, the
joys of neighbourliness are not always
unmixed, and this is the basic situation in tonight's
play. When it was first shown in *Comedy Playhouse*
last year 'Beggar My Neighbour' (by Ken Hoare
and Mike Sharland) proved very much to the public
taste; so much so that a new series of seven shows
with the same characters was put in hand.

That starts next week. Tonight the neighbours
are reintroduced in a repeat of the original production and this is the position: Gerald and Rose
Garvey (Peter Jones and June Whitfield) live next
door in Muswell Hill to Harry and Lana Butt (Reg
Varney and Pat Coombs). The wives are sisters,
which might be a very happy circumstance, except
for the fact that Gerald is an underpaid junior
executive and he and Rose are chronically broke,
while Harry is an opulent fitter.

Nonetheless, the Garveys are determined not to
lose face to the Butts. So when Harry, after having
rubbed their noses (figuratively speaking) in his
new 200-guinea colour TV set, goes on to boast
about his many foreign holidays, Gerald decides on
the spur of the moment to go one better. He
[announces] that he and Rose are just off for
[a holiday in the sunny] ... [of the Riviera]

The Garveys versus . . .

. . the Butts

PETER JONES
JUNE WHITFIELD
REG VARNEY
PAT COOMBS

BEGGAR MY NEIGHBOUR
BEGGAR MY NEIGHBOUR

TELEVISION CENTRE
SUNDAY 26TH MARCH 1967
DOORS OPEN 7.30 PM
NO ADMITTANCE AFTER 7.45 PM

COMPLIMENTARY TICKET
NOT FOR SALE

BBC tv

CHILDREN
UNDER 10
NOT ADMITTED

Beggar My Neighbour

This comedy series, with Reg Varney, Pat Coombs and Peter Jones (opposite) and (later) Desmond Walter-Ellis (above), was a joy to be in. It was directed by the brilliant David Croft. Pat and I played sisters. My husband was an underpaid junior executive and hers was a well-paid fitter in the same north London firm. We looked down on them, but they had the money. They had the car, we had the bicycles. On our first day of filming Peter and I were presented with bikes – I hadn't ridden one since childhood. We set off with a distinct wobble.

What's a
Mother For?

Dear Mona Washbourne, a unique
actress and a pleasure to work with.
Joe Brown, a top entertainer, turned out
to be an excellent actor as well. Such a
shame we can no longer enjoy Armchair
Theatre productions on our TV.

June Whitfield and Patrick Cargill in Father, Dear Father

Tommy Cooper and Patrick Cargill

(Above) A one-off Tommy Cooper sketch from *Life With Cooper*. He'd bring tricks to rehearsal to get a reaction from us all. Funny, funny man – the comics' comic. (Above right) Giving dancing lessons to Patrick Cargill in *Father, Dear Father*.

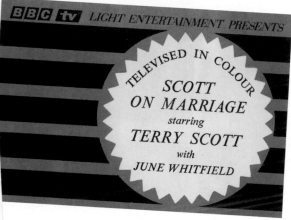

Terry Scott

I first worked with Terry in 1969 on his 'Scott On...' series. Peter Whitmore, the director, thought we could extend the domestic sketch which occurred each week into a sitcom, hence *Happy Ever After* in 1974 and then *Terry & June* in 1979. We worked together over a period of twenty years, with over a hundred HEA's and T&J's. When asked about our relationship (people did think we were married) Terry would say: 'We get on really well, there's nothing we wouldn't do for each other. I do nothing for her and she does nothing for me.' You can't work together for so long as we did without liking each other. I loved working with Terry, and Tim and Suzy also became friends with the Scott family. Critics found the show too cosy, middle-class and middle-everything. But the viewers rather enjoyed our 107 episodes. A regular audience of more than 10 million wasn't bad.

(Opposite) A Christmas episode of
Terry & June, joined (centre) by our
director Peter Whitmore. Below are
three picture of Terry as an angel
taken in Ravenscourt Park during
a break in filming for an episode of
'Scott On...' Peter Butterworth and
Frank Thornton were also dressed
in female attire and I remember the
three of them going to the pub for
lunch without changing.

Terry and his Stunts

(Opposite) Filming *Terry & June*. In this episode his boss has urged him to enter the world of politics and Terry is canvassing with a megaphone for election to his local council, from the top of a car which I'm driving. He used to do many of his own stunts, spectacularly falling into water time after time. This time he did allow a stunt man to take over, when the car came to a sudden stop, catapulting him into the water below.

(Above) I hadn't been on a horse for years. I ached a bit afterwards, but all in the good cause of filming.

Beautiful Bournemouth

These pictures are publicity shots for *A Bedfull of Foreigners* summer season in beautiful Bournemouth. (Opposite above) With the Town Crier at the RNLI. We took a trip in a lifeboat from Poole. Most exciting.

The Best Things in Life

The Best Things in Life (1969–70) with Harry H. Corbett,
a splendid method actor. Rather than Stanislavski, I go along
with Noël Coward's approach: 'Learn your lines and don't
bump into the furniture.' Different attitudes but equally
effective. The show was set in an office and the other girls
egged me on in my pursuit of him. Every week they'd say:
'If this doesn't get him, nothing will.' Oh, dear!

June not keen to "go solo"

JUNE WHITFIELD has been almost every comedian's wife, mother, daughter or girl friend at one time or another.

Jimmy Edwards, Benny Hill, Peter Sellers, Arthur Askey, Eric Sykes — you name them, she has helped them all to get their laughs, and has occasionally been known to steal the show—unwittingly of course.

She totted up the number the other day, and made it at least 20.

So convincingly does she adapt herself to any comedy part that Jimmy Edwards' recent tele-

TV Personality
by a
Special Correspondent

vision series became as much the Seven Faces of June as of Jim.

It was the same in the first of Benny Hill's current series. In the space of half-an-hour we saw her as a cockney flower-girl, a Kensington deb, a simpering Miss and seductive vamp.

"I'D HATE IT"

Here, you would think, was potentiality for a comedy series of her own. But mention the possibility to June Whitfield and she recoils in horror.

"I should hate it," she told me vehemently. "I couldn't stand the responsibility of a series of my own.

"I think there are very few women who can carry off a comedy series on television. You must have a strong personality so that whatever you say people will lap it up, or else you have to have an act.

"Dora Bryan could probably do it successfully, but then you have only to look at Dora's face

JUNE WHITFIELD

and hear her croaky voice to laugh. There's nothing funny about me."

I couldn't have agreed more. Small and slender, she was looking very attractive in well-fitting striped pants and sweater.

Hers is not the sort of face that off-screen makes you laugh, but it does make you look a second time, partly for its flawless complexion, partly for its halo of blonde hair, but mainly for her eyes, which are very blue, very bright and always look as though they are on the brink of laughter.

liked to do something where I got a great ovation. Anybody would, but so few women can do that."

June has not always been a comedian's "feed." She has played in musical comedy and straight plays in the theatre, and has also appeared in films.

She now does only television and sound radio, which fit more easily into a domestic routine.

HARD TO BE SERIOUS

After working with more than 20 comedians, June finds it difficult to play a straight part.

"When appearing in straight drama I have often found myself in the same situation as in comedy, and it has been an awful temptation not to play for a laugh.

"In any case," said the girl who made Ron Glum's long-suffering sweetheart, Eth, a national figure of fun. "I would rather do something to make people laugh than to send them into the depth of gloom."

QUITE CONTENT

"I couldn't make a funny crack and expect people to laugh," she went on, determined to make her limitations clear. "I am the one who says the line before the comedian's crack."

One thing is obvious, June Whitfield is quite content to stay one line below top billing.

"I was never a dedicated actress," she laughed, "and in any case, my career has to take second place to my marriage."

She is married to Timothy Aitchison, a surveyor, and they have a daughter, Susan, who is nearly two.

It was in the real life role of wife and mother that I met June Whitfield in her Bayswater home, and it is her favourite part.

Susan has the same fair colouring as her mother and, like her, seems to find life a great deal of fun. She looks like being another comedienne in the making.

If there is one thing June Whitfield is serious about, it is marriage. As she says, "It is far more likely to run into snags when a woman's career is put first and, after all, marriage lasts longer than a career.

BIG CHANGE

"I did start my career with a certain amount of ambition—I was intrigued with the mystery of the theatre—but it seems to have changed so much even in the time I have known it. It is so much more a commercial set-up now.

"I'm certainly not a thwarted actress. I am quite satisfied with what I do. I look on it merely as a very, pleasant way of making money.

("I suppose I should have

4—OXFORD MAIL, Friday, March 2, 1962

A foil for all the funny men

JUNE Whitfield has been almost every comedian's wife, mother, daughter or girl friend at one time or another. Jimmy Edwards, Benny Hill, Peter Sellers, Arthur Askey, Eric Sykes—she has helped them all to get their laughs, and has occasionally been known to steal the show—unwittingly, of course. She totted up the number the other day and made it at least 20.

So convincingly does she adapt herself to any comedy part, that Jimmy Edwards'

TV Personality
By Elsie Smith

recent television series became as much the seven faces of June as of Jim. It was the same in the first of Benny Hill's current series. In the space of half an hour we saw her as a Cockney flower-girl, a Kensington deb, a simpering miss and seductive vamp.

Here, you would think, was potentiality for a comedy series of her own. But mention the possibility to June Whitfield and she recoils in horror.

"I should hate it," she told me vehemently "I couldn't stand the responsibility of a series of my own.

"I think there are very few women who can carry off a comedy series on television. You must have a strong personality so that people will accept whatever you say, or else you have to have an act.

"Dora Bryan could probably do it successfully but then you have only to look at Dora's face and hear her croaky voice to laugh. There's nothing funny about me."

I couldn't have agreed more. Small and slender, she was looking very attractive in well-fitting striped pants and sweater.

Fine features

Hers is not the sort of face that off-screen makes you laugh but it does make you look a second time, partly for its flawless complexion and its halo of blond hair but mainly for her eyes which are very blue, very bright and always look as though they are on the brink of laughter

"I couldn't make a funny crack and expect people to laugh," she went on, determined to make her limitations clear. "I am the one who says the line before the comedian's crack."

One thing is obvious, June Whitfield is quite content to stay one line below top billing.

"I was never a dedicated actress," she laughed "and in any case my career has to take second place to by marriage."

She is married to surveyor Timothy Aitchison and they have a daughter, Susan, who is nearly two. It was in the real life role of wife and mother that I met June in her Bayswater home and it is her favourite part.

Susan has the same fair colouring as her mother and like her, seems to find life a great deal of fun. She looks like being another comedienne in the making.

If there is one thing June Whitfield is serious about, however, it is marriage. As she says: "It is far more likely to run into snags when a woman's career is put first and, after all, marriage lasts longer than a career.

"I did start my career with a certain amount of ambition —I was intrigued with the mystery of the theatre—but the theatre seems to have changed so much even in the time I have known it. It is so much more a commercial set-up now.

Satisfaction

"I'm certainly not a thwarted actress. I am quite satisfied with what I do. I look on it merely as a very pleasant way of making money. I suppose I should have liked to do something where I got a great ovation. Anybody would, but so few women can do that."

June has not always been a comedian's "feed." She has played in musical comedy and straight plays in the theatre, and has also appeared in films.

After working with more than 20 comedians, June finds it difficult to play a straight part.

"When appearing in straight drama I have found myself in the same situation as in comedy and it has been an awful temptation not to play for a laugh.

"In any case," said the girl who made Ron Glum's long suffering sweetheart, Eth, a national figure of fun. "I would rather do something to make people laugh than to send them into the depth of gloom."

JUNE WHITFIELD

June is busting out all over!

WHEN RADIO'S "Take It From Here" was the nation's comedy tonic, there was that 'Eth girl, remember? For seven years Miss June Whitfield played Dick Bentley's ghastly sweetheart.

Now suddenly Miss Whitfield bursts into vision, in "Beggar My Neighbour," in the B.B.C.'s big-time comedy slot, exactly where "Till Death Us Do Part," brought wealth and fame to its players.

All warm of heart, I went to welcome Miss Whitfield back into the light. Turning up her china-blue eyes from the level of my chest, she roundly told me:

"Don't you dare say at last I've been recognised by the telly boys! I've been on TV in sketches with Arthur Askey and Jimmy Edwards,

By KENNETH BAILY

though usually wearing wigs and spectacles."

Already her "Rose" in "Beggar My Neighbour" —she plays the wife of Peter Jones, an impoverished junior executive— promises to become a household name. And, more than that, I can reveal that none other than Tony Hancock

has asked June to partner him in his new TV series bid, due in a month or two.

The acclaim and riches tailing to good TV comedy players these days could put Miss Whitfield in the same class of limelight as bathed her star rôles in the stage musicals, "Love from Judy" and "South Pacific," when she was 26.

Now, at 37, having collected Tim, her surveyor husband; Susan, a six-year-old daughter; a very English house and garden in Wimbledon; and staidly English holidays by a sailing river in Hampshire, Miss Whit-

AT 37...SHE'S SUDDENLY A STAR AGAIN

field can talk calmly about the problem of her talent.

"It's true that comedy actresses—and, please, I am not a 'comic'—are a bit lacking on TV," she says.

"I really do have an awful feeling that to other women a lady being daft on the telly appears an undignified jibe at their sex.

It's a team

"We are getting on so well that already the B.B.C. is talking of keeping us together for a second series."

Miss Whitfield went back into her rehearsal with her happy team. A bespectacled director, who looked as serious as a surgeon, coldly told Reg Varney to give June a kiss.

Mr. Varney, of the letter-box lips, heaved his shoulders over a suppliant-looking June in his arms.

This done, with both their faces concentrated in hard thought, they turned their backs

"And, of course, until you really win them over, men want their TV women just to be dewy, soft and emotional.

"The great chance for funny actresses now is in these B.B.C. situation comedy series, where you are not out there on your own.

"It's teamwork, especially in a tight foursome like 'Beggar My Neighbour,' with such fine

artistes as Peter Jones, Reg Varney and Pat Coombs.

on each other, grabbed scripts and studied the next lines.

They may be great teammates, but no nervous energy is spent on B.B.C. rehearsal kisses. The director times them with a stop-watch, anyway.

Such precisely worked-out operations make a kiss hilarious on screen. And may give June Whitfield a TV stardom to outshine all memories of 'Eth.

● Bursting into vision— talented June Whitfield in the star comedy spot as Rose in "Beggar My Neighbour."

LOVELY JUNE IS LAUGHTER LINE LINK

By Elsie M. Smith

JUNE Whitfield has been almost every comedian's wife, mother, daughter or girl friend at one time or another. Jimmy Edwards, Benny Hill, Peter Sellars, Arthur Askey, Eric Sykes—you name them, she has helped them all to get their laughs, and has occasionally been known to steal the show — unwittingly, of course. She totted up the number the other day and made it at least 20.

So convincingly does she adapt herself to any comedy part, that Jimmy Edwards' recent television series became as much The Seven Faces of June as of Jim It was the same in the first of Benny Hill's current series. In the space of half an hour we saw her as a Cockney flower-girl, a Kensington deb, a simpering miss and seductive vamp.

Here, you would think, was potentiality for a comedy series of her own. But mention the possibility to June Whitfield and she recoils in horror.

NOT ON HER OWN

"I should hate it," she told me vehemently. "I couldn't stand the responsibility of a series on my own. I think there are very few women who can carry o... a comedy series on television. You must have a strong personality so that whatever you say people will lap it up, or else you have to have an act.

"Dora Bryan could probably do it sucessfully but then you have only to look at Dora's face and hear her croaky voice to laugh. There's nothing funny about me."

I couldn't have agreed more. Small and slender, she was looking very atractive in well fitting striped pants and sweater. Hers is not the sort of face that off-screen makes you laugh but it does make you look a second time, partly for its flawless complexion, partly for its halo of blonde hair but mainly for her eyes which are very blue, very bright and always look as though they are on the brink of laughter.

QUITE CONTENT

One thing is obvious. June Whitfield is quite content to stay one line below top billing.

She is married to surveyor Timothy Aitchison and they have a daughter. Susan, who is nearly two. It was in the real life role of wife and mother that I met June Whitfield in her Bayswater home and it is her favourite part.

If there is one thing June Whitfield is serious about, it is marriage. As she says: "It is far more likely to run into snags when a woman's career is put first and, after all,

June Whitfield

"I did start my career with a certain amount of ambition — I was intrigued with the mystery of the theatre — but it seems to have changed so much even in the time I have known it. It is so much more a commercial set-up now.

"I'm certainly not a thwarted actress. I am quite satisfied with what I do. I look on it merely as a very pleasant way of making money. I suppose I should have liked to do something where I got a great ovation, anybody would, but so few women can do that."

STRAIGHT PARTS

June has not always been a comedian's "feed." She has played in musical comedy and straight plays in the theatre, and has also appeared in films. She now does only television and sound radio, which fit more easily into a domestic routine.

After working with more than 20 comedians, June finds it difficult to play a straight part.

"When appearing in straight drama I have often found myself in the same situation as in comedy and it has been an awful temptation not to play for a laugh."

"In any case", said the girl who made Ron Glum's long suffering sweetheart, Eth, a national figure of fun, "I would rather do something to make people laugh than to send them into the dep..."

Anyone But Me

These cuttings speak for themselves. My early desire to hide behind wigs, glasses and character voices stayed with me until I did *The Best Things in Life*. I was terrified of appearing as myself. Age has improved my confidence. Ronnie Barker said he felt the same. He was a wigs, glasses and voices man – and how!

Chapter Six

'OH, LOOK–THERE GOES AN ADVERT'

Suzy – Growing Up

(Opposite above) Suzy, about to take part in a school play, with her admiring parents. I hope she didn't have to move much. (Below left) Mum with Suzy. (Below right) Suzy as a schoolgirl in front of the annexe we were rebuilding for my Mum.

Do Me a Favour

This was a sitcom pilot from LWT which sadly went no
further. Written by Len Walker and directed by William
G. Stewart, it had well-known actors in Peter Jones and
Terence Alexander.

The Magnificent Seven Deadly Sins

With Harry Secombe in this 1971 film, which was made up of seven separate stories, each written by different writers and directed by Graham Stark. The episode I appeared in was 'Envy' and in one scene I was having a bubble bath. Graham was livid because the bubbles wouldn't bubble. He kept swishing the water hopefully with his hand, while shouting at the prop man. He got some very funny looks from the crew, who were unaware that I was modestly wearing an unseen swimsuit.

From Outer Space?

A Tale of Two Microbes was a twenty-minute educational documentary. It was sponsored by Unilever for domestic science classes in schools and written by Frank Muir and Jeff Inman. As Basil and Desdemona Salmonella, Frank and I travelled at lightning speed from shop to kitchen, leaving millions of baby salmonellas in our wake to contaminate whatever they touched. This was of course before everyone was aware of sell-by dates. It wasn't easy to keep a straight face.

Frank and Denis

I never tired of Frank and Denis's 'misinterpretation' of words.
For example, Eth: 'Oh Ron, when are we getting married? You'll
never know how much I yearn.' Ron: 'I do, Eth and it's not enough
for us both to live on.'

(Below) Frank and Denis listening to a rehearsal, prepared for
script changes if required.

by Frank Muir and Denis Norden

The men behind radio's funniest half-hour

MUIR AND NORDEN, who also write the script for The Seven Faces of Jim, return the compliment.
"June," says Frank Muir, 'always understands what we are getting at and gets more out of it than we put in. She is the answer to a scriptwriter's prayer. She is phenomenal."

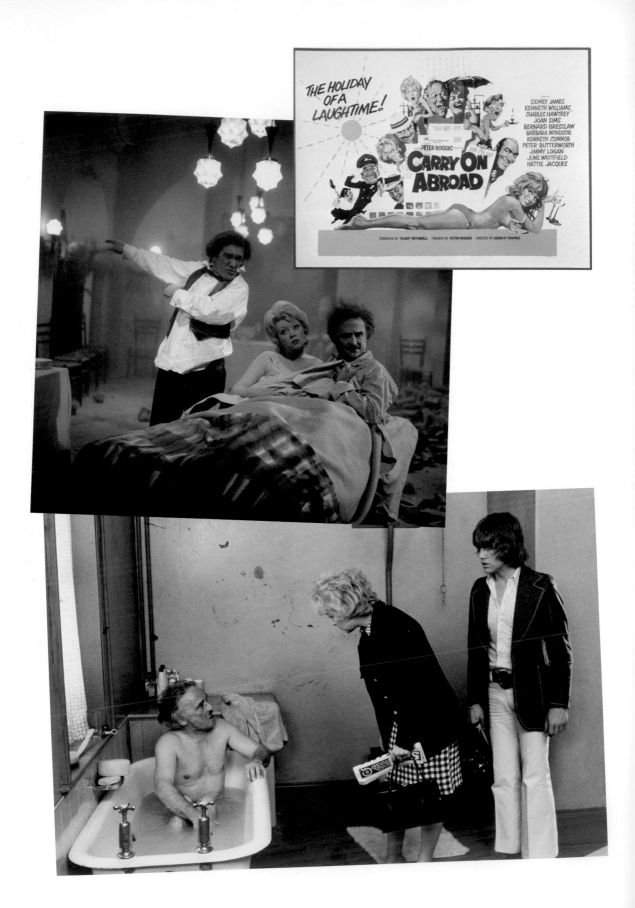

Carry On Abroad

My favourite 'Carry On...'. I was usually paired with the delightful Ken Connor. (Opposite above) Peter Butterworth, with Ken and me in the bed, a publicity shot. In the film Ken jumped on the bed with me in it and the whole thing fell through to the floor below. Luckily it worked on the first take. (Above top) Two Kens, Connor and Williams, on the Wundatours coach taking us to the tour hotel in Ellsbells. (Above left) The prudish Mrs Blunt (me) in a clinch with Ray Brooks.

(Opposite below) *Carry On Girls*. I was a feminist councillor who confronted the local mayor, Ken, in the bath.

Bless This House

Once again, in this 1972 film, I was married to Terry Scott. This time we were Ronald and Vera Baines. We moved in next door to Sid and Jean Abbott (Sid James and Diana Coupland). The usual comedy mix-ups, with neighbours hating each other, including a food fight in a café and finally young lovers united, married and living happily ever after. The TV series was a long-running success.

SID JAMES
DIANA COUPLAND)
TERRY SCOTT
PETER BUTTERWORTH
SALLY GEESON
GEOFF RODWAY

"BLESS THIS HOUSE"
JUNE 1972.

In *Bless This House* Terry and I are seeking a truce with our
neighbours Diana Coupland, Sid James and their daughter
Sally Geeson.

Romance With a Double Bass

This was a comedy by John Cleese (below right) and Connie Booth, involving a princess and a double bass player. I played the princess's mother. We filmed in the magnificent Wilton House near Salisbury. Denis Ramsden played my husband. We were chatting one day and I asked him what his next job was. It turned out he was joining Terry Scott in *A Bedfull of Foreigners* on tour in South Africa. I was also in the cast and it was a delight to meet Denis, also known as 'Slim', before we set off on tour.

A Bedfull of Foreigners

The 1975 tour of South Africa of this bedroom farce by Dave Freeman was fascinating. We started in Cape Town at the Nico Malan Theatre, the first play to visit after mixed-race audiences were allowed. We had a great cast and all enjoyed each other's company. Terry's children joined us, as did Lynda Baron's, and Suzy came to visit as well when we were in Durban.

The Hilton Playhouse

"A BEDFULL OF FOREIGNERS"
By Dave Freeman

Souvenir

The Hilton Playhouse presents
'A Bedfull of Foreigners'

A bedfull of laughs

Miss June Whitfield, that accomplished comedienne with the superb sense of timing and humour, has a date in Hongkong.

She is to star in the Hilton Playhouse production of "A Bedfull of Foreigners," which opens on September 15.

Miss Whitfield's past list of co-stars reads like a Who's Who of comic celebrities. They include Jimmy Edwards, Dick Bentley, Tony Hancock, Joyce Grenfell, Benny Hill, Leslie Crowther, Ronnie Barker, Stanley Baxter, Frankie Howerd, Harry Corbett and Terry Scott.

And appearing with her in the laugh-a-minute comedy in Hongkong will be Terry Scott, Aimi Macdonald, Dilys Laye, Dennis Ramsden, Jimmy Thompson and Anthony Morton.

'A Bedfull of Foreigners'

Two favourites of the London theatre and television scene, Terry Scott and June Whitfield, are among a cast of seven signed by Hongkong Hilton manager, Mr Philip Mermod for the Hilton's next Playhouse presentation from September 16 to 30.

The play, "A Bedfull of Foreigners" is an hilarious comedy set in a bedroom of a small French hotel. Terry Scott and June Whitfield starred in the successful 15-month run in the West End which seen here discussing signing of the contra

---

The Hilton Playhouse presents Dave Freeman's spicy Bedroom Comedy in a new extended entertainment season!

Terry Scott · June Whitfield
Aimi Macdonald · Dilys Laye
with
Dennis Ramsden · Anthony Morton
and
Jimmy Thompson
in

A BEDFULL OF FOREIGNERS
A NEW COMEDY BY DAVE FREEMAN

"Classically Funny" — Daily Telegraph
"Genuinely Hilarious" — The Guardian
Direct From Duke of York's Theatre, London.

British airways

HONGKONG HILTON

場劇頓爾希
劇喜默幽演

一部充滿英式幽默的喜劇《
滿床春色》將於九月十六日起在
香港希爾頓酒店劇院公演。

電視片集
利史葛及鐘茵韋菲
主角為在英國甚有名氣之泰

克公爵劇院公演時，
演期達十五個月之久
，演員除了男女主角
丹尼士藍斯頓、迪
莉、占美湯遜及安
東尼摩頓等著名英國
舞台演員，

外。
尚有愛瑪麥奴
均享有盛
聲，此劇約
在英國約

，劇情風趣幽默。
劇作家迪夫費曼名作
《滿林春色》為

New light-hearted play in town soon

JUNE WHITFIELD

DILYS LAYE

AIMI MacDONALD

TERRY SCOTT

WHAT probably will be the year's final summer road show here will be held the week after this coming one by the Hilton Playhouse productions.

The play, which should be light and laughter-provoking as the title alone suggests, is A Bedfull of Foreigners. It will start on Friday, September 16 and will run nightly from 7 pm at the hotel's Grand Ballroom up to month's end, except on Sunday, September 18 and Thursday, September 29.

The main characters of the play are June Whitfield, Terry Scott, Dilys Laye, and Aimi MacDonald.

June has been around the circuit for sometime, appearing in plays, films, pantomime, revue, repertory and musicals. She has concentrated on TV, radio and films lately, but she is looking forward to returning to the theatre again.

June has been in Bedfull since it opened in 1976 at the Victoria Palace and Duke of York theatres, working Terry Scott since 1969 on TV's Scott on...

Bedfull of Foreigners was specially written for Terry by Dave Freeman. But he has been a favourite on stage and TV before that, and films, too, particularly the Carry On series. He also created the character James Harris in The Mating Game.

Aimi is Scottish, started out as a dancer, became a Paris and Las Vegas showgirl, and by chance landed a small part in On the Town. From there she graduated effortlessly to a succession of "dizzy blonde" roles West End musicals, and then to a host of lead roles. She now has her own cabaret show.

Dily's Laye is also a familiar face among Carry On disciples, although she has been a success in may other stage plays as well as other films, as the Countess of Hongkong.

Hong Kong

In 1977 we were invited to take *Bedfull* to the Hong Kong Hilton for three weeks for their Dinner Theatre. The man lunching with Terry and me (opposite) is the general manager of the hotel. The weather was not as hot as the summer before in England, when we were playing at the Victoria Palace and also rehearsing our TV show during the day.

THIS IS
YOUR LIFE

JUNE WHITFIELD

This book is
presented to

JUNE WHITFIELD

as a memento of
her appearance as
guest of honour on

This Is Your Life

19th March, 1976
Thames Television, London.

This is Your Life

Tim and I were on holiday in Suffolk. He said he had to get home earlier than we had planned, for a meeting. To my, 'But they know you're away', he replied: 'Yes, but this is important.' I found out later it was a meeting with Thames TV about my *This is Your Life*. He had been sworn to secrecy of course and didn't want to spoil the surprise. When it happened, in March 1976, 'My flabber', as Frankie Howerd might have said, 'was never so ghasted.' As I had been surprised by Eamonn Andrews at home, I was at least able to change clothes before being whisked off to the studio.

Muff and Suzy thoroughly enjoyed the occasion –
the Thames TV letter to Muff is reproduced opposite.
How we wished Dad could have been with us, he'd
have been so proud.

Thames Television

Thames Television Limited
306-316 Euston Road
London NW1 3BB
01-387 9494

Mrs. B.G. Whitfield,
C/O The Eardley Hotel,
Worthing,
Sussex.

15th March, 1976.

Dear Georgina,

"THIS IS YOUR LIFE"

We are delighted that you will be able to join us for the programme on Friday 19th March.

I have had a chat with Tim on the telephone and made arrangements with him, and I said I would drop you a line to tell you the arrangements.

I have arranged for a car to come and collect you from home on Friday at 1.30 p.m. which will be after June has left the house, to bring you to our studios at the above address for the afternoon rehearsal. Would you please bring with you at this time whatever you wish to wear for the programme as there will be a dressing room and time for you to change here.

Tim and Susie will be here for the morning rehearsal, and they will then have to go home for the afternoon.

After you have changed we will have drinks before the programme starts at 6.45 p.m. I hope it will be alright for you to bring a little case with you in the car with your dress in, and for you to stay with us at the studios until we record the show.

After the show we should be pleased if you would join us for a playback in order that you may see the programme in its entirety. Drinks will be served before the programme and a buffet meal will be provided afterwards A car will then be available to take you all home together to Wimbledon.

I do hope you are having a good time in Worthing. Could I please just ask you to take great care that June does not see this letter if you take it back to London with you.

I look forward to meeting you on Friday. With best wishes.

Yours sincerely,

Debi Black

Debi Black,
Programme Organiser,
"THIS IS YOUR LIFE"

The Cast List, in No Order of Billing

Some of the kind souls who turned up for my 'Life' (opposite, clockwise from top left): Terry Scott, Bob Monkhouse, Arthur Askey, Reg Varney, Charlie Drake, Frankie Howerd, Peter Butterworth, Dick Bentley. (Above) Frank and Denis, who were unable to attend but were caught on camera kindly raising a glass, made flattering remarks. It was such an emotional day.

(Opposite above) Leslie Crowther and Ronnie Barker. (Opposite below) Bob Monkhouse and Peter Butterworth look on as I greet my cousin Verena who had come all the way from New Zealand. When she received the phone call one night and was asked, 'Are you June Whitfield's cousin?', her first thoughts were that I must have died. She was relieved, I'm glad to say, when she learned the reason for the call.

(Below) Behind me is Verena's brother Richard and between Suzy and Tim, my brother John. Next to Tim is Muff. Also present: Terry Scott, Lynda Baron, Pat Coombs, Peter Jones, Reg Varney and many other old friends. I also had a video message from Jimmy Edwards and Eric Sykes from South Africa, where they were on tour with *Big Bad Mouse*.

The Birds Eye Ads

Between 1969 and 1981 I took part in about 20 advertisements for Birds Eye frozen foods, in various disguises (above and opposite). When asked if I had made the delicious food myself, I would reply yes and receive a disbelieving look in return. The voice-over was always: 'Birds Eye pie can make a dishonest woman of you.' The ads were created by the Collet Dickinson Pearce agency and were directed like little films, not surprisingly as the future Hollywood film directors Ridley Scott and Alan Parker were involved in some of them. Those registering disbelief were Terry Thomas, Harry H. Corbett, Frank Thornton, Herbert Lom and Julian Orchard.

These ads were on TV while Terry and I were rehearsing at the BBC for *Terry & June*. Driving into the BBC one day there was a group of fans waiting for *Top of the Pops*. As I passed, one shouted, 'Oh, look – there goes an advert.'

Chapter Seven
BACK TO PANTO

It Ain't Half Hot Mum

This was one of three shows about the
Second World War written by David Croft
and Jimmy Perry – the others were *Dad's
Army* and *'Allo, 'Allo!* In this episode
Michael Knowles and I climbed a tree via
an unseen ladder which was then removed.
We waited breathlessly for rather a long
time before we realized the rest of the cast
were having a tea break. They eventually
came back laughing and helped us down.
(Opposite top, from the left) Michael
Knowles, me, Jimmy Perry and Donald Hewlett.
(Above) Flanking me are Donald Hewlett and Windsor Davies.

Dick Emery's Christmas Show, 1980

Dick Emery, what a giggler. I did several sketches with Dick, we were usually a husband and wife who hated each other – even tried to poison each other – but were all smiles when anyone else appeared. Dick was so funny and always tried to make me laugh in the middle of a sketch – he often succeeded.

(Below) The 1980 Royal Variety Show at the London Palladium, being presented to the Queen Mother, a thrilling moment. Left to right: Terry Scott, Gordon Jackson and Penelope Keith.

Mike Yarwood in Persons

No, that's not him opposite – it's me as Maggie Thatcher, playing
Juliet. Mike Yarwood was Ted Heath, playing Romeo. (Above)
Meeting the lady herself, with June Mendoza, a friend and much-
sought-after artist, who has painted Lady Thatcher.

Chichester
Festival
Theatre·

Frankie Howerd
AS
Simple Simon
June Whitfield
AS THE
Vegetable Fairy
in
JACK and the
BEANSTALK

with
Terence Conoley · Maria Friedman
Gay Soper · Ken Wilson · Aubrey Woods

Directed by Roger Redfarn

Choreography by Lindsay Dolan
Music directed by Ian Hughes   Lighting by Bill Bray

17th December to 15th January
Matinees 2.30pm   Evenings 7.30pm

Children and OAPs half price
Party reductions and special pre-Christmas prices

BOX OFFICE: CHICHESTER 781312

Jack and the Beanstalk with Frankie Howerd

Frankie Howerd brought me back to pantomime, at Chichester in
1982. Tim and I and Frank and Dennis, his manager, became good
friends. In the years that followed, Frank would phone and ask,
'What are you doing on Thursday?' If 'Nothing' was the reply he'd
say, 'I'll be round for dinner at 8 with Betty [his sister] and Dennis.'
He loved 'going to the dogs' – we often went to White City and then,
after White City closed, to Wimbledon dog track.

JACK and the BEANSTALK

by John Morley

The Villagers and Beanpeople with Lindsay Dolan. Left to right:
Michael Leno, Roland Brine, Fiona Scoones, Mark Hutchinson,
Lesley Guinn, Nick Raymond, Deborah Snook and Lynn Emeny.

Jack and the Beanstalk was my first panto since 1948! I was
Cinderella then, but the Vegetable Fairy in 1982 – well, fairies
have no age limit. I appeared in panto again in 1983 with
Roy Hudd and Jack Tripp – a very dainty Dame, the opposite
of Terry Scott's raunchy one. My final panto was in 1994 with
Rolf Harris.

(Top left) Emerging from the scenery during rehearsals.
(Top right) Aubrey Woods as Fleshcreep, the Giant's henchman.
(Above left) Gay Soper on stage, with the scenery being painted
in the background. (Above right) Shirley Read making last-
minute adjustments to my costume.

'We sang "Spread a little happiness". Frank certainly did.'

Dick Whittington with Roy Hudd

In the interval Roy and I would make up little verses for the end of the show, referring to some coach-load in the audience. Roy told me he was worried about finding a replacement for Alison Steadman, who was leaving *The News Huddlines*. He said they'd tried everyone. I said, 'You haven't tried me!' 'But you have to impersonate politicians and famous people,' he said. At the next performance I introduced the fight between Dick and Queen Rat (Honor Blackman – opposite, above) in my best Margaret Thatcher voice: 'Go to your corners – oh, isn't this exciting – and when you hear the bell, come out fighting!' Roy said, 'You've got the job!'

OBE

Great excitement in 1985 as Her Majesty the Queen
honoured me with an OBE, the Order of the British
Empire (Old But Energetic?). (Below left) All spruced up
for the occasion, with the security guards searching the
cars just in case... Her Majesty was gracious as always
and having received my OBE I joined the others being
honoured in the magnificent room where a military
band was playing. I particularly remember their
rendering of 'If I Were a Rich Man'. We all felt rich
that day.

(Right) Taking part in a TV sketch with Basil Brush – it was rather odd talking to and dancing for a fox… (Below) Must have been a birthday.

A Freeman of the City

Becoming a Freeman of the City of London at the Guildhall. Swearing allegiance to the Queen and proud to do so.

Animals in the Family

Our delightful bunny called Guti. I believe he was
from a Dutch family of rabbits, 'Agutis'. Tim arrived
home with him one day and I could see why. Guti was
enchanting. Tim would sit him on the desk and Guti
would shred paper (see opposite). (Above) Tim asleep,
pipe in hand, with Sid our Labrador behaving like a
puppy, and me with a visiting friend. Sid was with us
from puppyhood until he was 13, which is good going
for a Labrador. We missed him so much.

A Dog Called Rabbit

Although Sid was happy to have Guti sitting on his back, our next dog Rabbit (left), a cross between a Tibetan Terrier and a Jack Russell, would have preferred to have eaten Guti. They were firmly kept apart. Rabbit (dog) had started his life with Jimmy Edwards. Jim was often in Australia and we 'babysat' Rabbit while he was away (dear old Sid had gone to the Doggy Kennels in the Sky). Jim had called the dog 'Rubu' and when Guti died Rubu became Rabbit – don't ask me why. He was a dear dog and was with us until he was 18.

Suzy

Our 'baby' is 21 years old. A good family party was held to celebrate
– aunts, uncles, cousins and friends from school and university. Suzy
wisely completed her education before becoming an actor. I advise
all would-be thespians to do the same.

BBC RADIO LIGHT ENTERTAINMENT

presents

Radio's Comic Weekly

starring

**ROY HUDD
JUNE WHITFIEL**
and **CHRIS EMME**

Music from
THE HUDDLINE

The BBC Radio Theatre
Broadcasting House
Portland Place, London W1

**THURSDAY
24th OCTOBER '96**
Doors open 12.45pm

THE NEWS HUDDLINES

starring **ROY HUDD**
Winner of the Lifetime Achievement In Radio Award
JUNE WHITFIELD and **CHRIS EMMETT**

Thursdays
4th, 11th, 18th, 25th May
1st, 8th, 15th, 22nd, 29th June & 6th July '95

At the Radio Theatre, Broadcasting House, Portland Place, London, W1
Doors open 12.45pm.

For tickets send
Radio Ticket Unit

Name: ....
Address: ....

Telephone Number: ....

Ref: **NH**

TODAY'S CHOICE

GILLIAN REYNOLDS

Still making the Huddlines

The News Huddlines *Radio 2: 7.00 - 7.30 pm*
Welcome back, dear Roy and all the Huddliners, to a 40th series which will do the nation a real service if it can raise laughs out of a creaking government, a persistent shortage of water in parts of the nation where it seldom stops raining and a royal family which can't move without tripping.

George Melly's Owning Up... *Radio 4: 11.00 - 11.30 pm*
This must have seemed like a good idea at the time. Dramatise George Melly's later biographical volume (not the one about naughty goings-on in the Navy) and bring in George himself ...eet- ...do ...t's ...not ...pro- ...than ...ded.

Chris Emmett, June Whitfield and Roy Hudd (Radio 2, 7.00 pm)

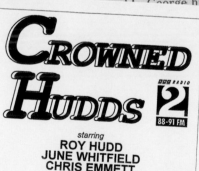

CROWNED HUDDS

BBC RADIO 2 88-91 FM

starring
**ROY HUDD
JUNE WHITFIELD
CHRIS EMMETT**

Dates
**17th, 22nd, 31st May
6th, 13th August** '95
at the
**Radio Theatre, Broadcasting House,
Portland Place, London W1**
(Doors open 7.15pm)
For FREE tickets send an SAE to: BBC Radio Ticket Unit, London W1A 4WW

Name: ....
Address: .... 1st Choice   No. of tickets
.... 2nd Choice
Ref: **CROWN**   3rd Choice

The News Huddlines

Sixteen happy and fun years I spent with Roy Hudd and
Chris Emmett in *The News Huddlines*, a topical radio show
which had already been on air for ten years before I joined
it in 1984. Every Thursday morning the scriptwriters would
meet and scour the papers for stories which were crying
out for 'mickey-taking'. What a feast they'd have had in
2009 with the credit crunch and MPs' expenses. I am often
asked, when is the *Huddlines* coming back? Apart from its
popularity it launched the careers of a number of writers.

(Above) Back row: Chris, Roy, Dirk Maggs, our producer, and Richard Clegg, announcer. Front row: Peter Moss in the flying jacket, a brilliant band leader and composer, me and Maureen Trotman, who looked after us all.

(Left) Recording the *Huddlines* at the old Paris Cinema in Lower Regent Street, the home of so many BBC radio shows. In 1995 the BBC's lease on the Paris expired and comedy shows moved to the Radio Theatre at Broadcasting House. We all missed the atmosphere and intimacy of the Paris. It was ideal for comedy.

Roy Hudd, Birthday Boy

(Above) Roy's 50th birthday. (Opposite, small photo)
Celebrating 25 years of *The News Huddlines*. In 2009,
Roy was given a lunch to celebrate 50 years in show
business. He is multi-talented – comic, raconteur, actor
and an unrivalled authority on music hall. I can listen
to him for hours.

Sabina Franklyn celebrates her birthday at the Theatre Royal with fellow members of the cast of The Rivals. Left to right are Christopher Strauli, Sabina, Suzy Aitchison and June Whitfield.

Family show for June

GAME show king Leslie Crowther will not be the only one playing for laughs in his Edwardian home at Corston this week — house guests June Whitfield and daughter Suzy are sure to raise a few smiles.

The comedy actress, best known for her television role with Terry Scott in Terry and June, is starring at Bath's Theatre Royal in Sheridan's The Rivals. Daughter Suzy Aitchison, 26, is teaming up with her mother on stage for the first time.

June and Leslie are old friends — they first met in 1959 in a variety playhouse — and keep in regular contact.

Calkin.

Suzy last appeared with her mother at the age of nine in a television sketch send-up of the Fairy Liquid advert, but their acting paths have not since crossed.

An acting career was cut out for Suzy almost from the moment she was born.

"I was never pushed into it, but the thought of not being an actress never crossed my mind," said Suzy.

She does not deny that having a famous mother has helped her at the start of her career.

"It does mean some doors open to me, but if I'm no good people aren't going to employ me."

At the moment most of her work seems to be in comedy like her mother, but she says she is not looking for the sort of comedy partnership June has with Terry Scott.

"I don't want to be just an echo of my mother," she says.

While her career is taking off, her mother admits she is winding down.

June, who won't give away her age but likes to be described as mature said, "I have got beyond being ambitious. I work because I love acting, I really don't like being away from home and my husband for very long."

Her schedule for the next few months looks anything but declining. She is starring in Christmas panto with Terry Scott, doing a regular spot on Radio Two's The News Huddlines with Roy Hudd, and another Terry and June series is planned for the spring.

A Rare Appearance Together

Sheridan's *The Rivals* in 1986. Me and Suzy in a play together, as Mrs Malaprop and Lucy the maid (opposite). In a following tour I was absent but Suzy was promoted to playing Lydia. The original production saw Clive Owen, now a famous film star, in a minor role.

An Ideal Husband

I first met Joanna Lumley in this play at Chichester in 1987.
Joanna was then living in Wimbledon, as I was, and she often
gave me a lift home after the show on a Saturday and back on
Monday. Jo is tall and elegant and the dearest person. We met
again of course in *Ab Fab*. More of that later. In the picture
below, from the left: Lucy Fleming, Clive Francis, William Fox,
David Gwillim and Amanda Waring, with Jo and me seated.

Cast snaps, mostly taken by me back stage, of the casts of
An Ideal Husband and *Ring Round the Moon*, which both
played at Chichester. (Opposite) Top row: Lucy Fleming,
William Fox and David Gwillim, Holly Aird, Jo Lumley;
middle row: Lucy Fleming, José Ferrer, Michael Siberry,
Linda Thorson; bottom row: Clive Francis, me, Christopher
Goodwin, Diana Marchment with Tom Kelly. (Above) Me and,
clockwise from top right, Diana Marchment, Madge Ryan,
Richard Avery and Tom Kelly.

Over My Dead Body

In this play Charles Routledge (opposite, bottom
left) was my dresser. What a character. He was
in his eighties but he was up and down endless
stairs to the 'wardrobe' at the Savoy Theatre every
night. He was Diana Rigg's dresser but she was
not working at the time. I said to him: 'You have
worked for some great stars, this is a bit of a
come down.' He replied, 'Oh well, you can't win
'em all.' We got on famously from then on.
Opposite, clockwise from top left: Donald Sinden,
me, Ken Wynne, Frank Middlemass and Charles.
(Below) Obviously a very important occasion!

When the Dons Won the Cup

In 1981 I had been asked to become president of the
Wimbledon Football supporters' club (I retired when
the club moved to Crystal Palace). When Wimbledon
beat Liverpool in the FA Cup Final in 1988 there was
huge excitement. It seemed that all Wimbledon turned
out to celebrate. Every pub overflowed onto the
streets. (Below) Enjoying a drink with friends in
eager anticipation before the match.

(Opposite) A family snap on Tim's 70th birthday.

Chapter Eight
THE ABSOLUTELY FABULOUS NINETIES

Hinge & Bracket

(Opposite) I joined the pianist and singer for an episode of their radio show. You certainly wouldn't recognise the two men beneath their disguises. They were a highly successful duo on radio and TV.

(Above) A panto promotion. Left to right: Roy, Jack Tripp and Debbie, second from right, who was soon to become Mrs Roy Hudd.

FILMING 19.6.'91
4 ABSOLUTELY FABULOUS

Jo, Jennifer and 'Mother'

I had taken part in a *French & Saunders* sketch and
Jennifer Saunders offered me the part of her mother
in *Ab Fab* – one small scene in the pilot. Jennifer said
if the show was commissioned, she would include
Mother. I laughed aloud when I read the script and
couldn't wait to be part of the show. I thought Mother
was a suburban housewife, but as the week went on
she became a kleptomaniac, was always able to get
into the house and turned out to be as mad as Eddy
and Patsy. She was determined not to miss anything
and was great fun to play. Opposite: Jo and Jennifer
(top) and with Julia Sawalha as Saffy (below).

Absolutely Fabu-less!

Littlehammer'94

N-icely does it

TORVILL and Dean face the music and dance live on TV as week two of the Winter Olympics starts. Here's when to tune in to see Britain's gold medal hopefuls.

● **SUNDAY:** Chris and Jayne perform their ice dance, the rumba (BBC2, 7pm, Eurosport 6pm.

● **MONDAY:** The moment of truth in the free dance, with Let's Face The Music And Dance.

Coach Betty Callaway says the routine has changed 50 per cent since it narrowly won them the European title last month.

But have they changed too much too quickly? Find out live (BBC1, 3pm, and highlights BBC1, 11.50pm, Eurosport from 9pm.

The women's skating pitches best girl Tonya Harding against good girl Nancy Kerrigan.

Tonya is accused of trying to get Nancy out of the Olympic running by plotting an attack on her knee with an iron bar.

See them battle for honours live on Ice (BBC1, 9pm).

● **WEDNESDAY:** Technical programmes (BBC2 highlights, 11.15pm, Eurosport 9am-6pm.

● **FRIDAY:** The free dance (BBC2, 8pm-2pm, Eurosport from 9pm).

Tanks a lot

A WIDOW finds her sofa is worth a must in ANTIQUES ROADSHOW (Sunday, BBC1, 5.35pm).

Jill Hobbs was clearing out bric-a-brac when a bed when she came across silver tankards, teapots and a "turban-dress" cup shaped like a ship's hull.

"I said I'd be happy to give it away," says Jill, who tripped over the collection in Peckham.

Instead she took the collection to Roadshow expert Ian Pickford and he advised her to insure it for £350,000.

One 17th century tank and was valued at £40,000, the ship's head cup at £18,000.

Jill, struggling on £85-a-week pension, says "I couldn't believe my ears. I met my Harold would have been here to see it."

All for nan

NEW EastEnders wheeler-dealer Wicksy, actor Michael French, has revealed his one regret about his big break on Albert Square.

Barkeeper Michael, 31, who plays Pat's long-lost son David, says "My nan died last year, and EastEnders was her favourite programme.

"So I put her picture in front of the telly when it's on."

Garry Bushell is on holiday—

WELL HEELED... June in patterned leggings £155, boots £695

WELL WRAPPED... pencil skirt £265, jacket £595, sweater £155, Wrap £745

By MATTHEW WRIGHT

BATTY TV mum June Whitfield proves she is really back in fashion as a cult hit.

The actress decided to luxuriate as a suburban wife in Terry And June to bask on top as a star in the trendiest hit of Gone all, **ABSOLUTELY FABULOUS**.

And to celebrate, The Sun kitted her out in the top Christian Lacroix clothes worn by screen daughter Jennifer Saunders.

June said: "The most outrageously thing about playing Mother is that most of the clothes I wear are my own."

"I don't throw my old outfits away because you never know when they are going to come in useful."

Expensive

"They are all good quality, years old so then always look that bit out of date.

"I've always been interested in fashion but I'm not a great one for buying designer clothes, they're too expensive. Three times my size, though, I don't think they'll be some.

I wouldn't pay £350 for posh leggings, it doesn't seem right, says Ju...

THAT'S LIFE
Tuesday, BBC1 9.00pm

ABSOLUTELY

Thursday, next, 9.00pm

think I'll be able to resist these leggings."

Then she noticed the £350 price tag and £inched. They were twice the price before the January sale.

June sighed: "The most expensive thing I've ever bought was a dress for £265.

"But I've got beautiful things but I don't think I'd pay so much for leggings. It doesn't seem right to me.

June, a leftish girl in Carry On films in the 1990s, is revelling in being in demand again at 68. She was on CELEBRITY SQUARES last night.

Victoria

"And I've....guests on The....all the time and I....back in the studio outside, which made me sigh at.... Britt & the.... Smirnoff and Jo....

PARTY

People as.... waste to get.... a new role I'll.... not front June.... I'm now wait.... to play like Jennifer.

"Ab-Fab.... June.... has been... humour to mak.... Terry....

Day I seduced Julian

JUNE has co-starred with all the comic greats, from Jimmy Edwards and Tony Hancock to the Carry On gang and Terry Scott.

But she's still in touch with the modern comedy scene. Her favourite stars are Harry Enfield and Rowan Atkinson.

She even has time to move controversial comics like Ben Elton and Julian Clary, her co-star in the last Carry On film, Carry On Columbus.

She said: "After filming, Julian told me he had a part for me in his new series. When he told me

the new..... started t.....

"We w.... of the S.... so I ask.... the ske....

ISSUE 159   FEBRUARY 19-25

Sun TV Super GUIDE

WORTH 70p   FREE WITH THE SUN

Ab Fab June is back in fashion
—PAGE 3

Casualty star who clobbered Clint
PAGE SEVEN

Day Anna wished she WASN'T there
PAGE SIX

CHRISTIAN LACROIX PARIS

Enjoy diet Coke

FEDS
The diet Coke Movie
Premiere - Tuesday, ITV, 8.30pm

FILMING ABFAB 9.1.'95

A Makeover

The Sun decided to give Mother a makeover,
as she was usually seen in somewhat boring
trousers and cardies (very often mine). So off
we went to Lacroix, Eddy's favourite couturier.
This was the result. I blotted my copybook in
the store by gasping at the price of a pair of
designer leggings. I thought £350 was out
of Mother's range.

Let's party, sweetie: Jennifer Saunders with June Whitfield and Jane Horrocks at the launch of Absolutely Fabulous in America

New York, a Stretch Limo and Concorde

(Above) The trip to New York with Jennifer and Jane Horrocks (Bubbles in *Ab Fab*). Joanna and Julia were working and couldn't join us. The reason for the trip was to attend an *Ab Fab* 'Lookalike Party'. The winner, of many dressed as Patsy, was a man about six-foot tall in high heels – looking more Patsy than Patsy. There were Eddys too, and I think I spotted one cardigan in the throng, which could have been Saffy or Mother! We were wined and dined, ferried about in a stretch limo and flew back on Concorde. Terrific. (Opposite, below) Bob Spiers, the director, with some of the cast.

MERRY AND JUNE

Much has been made of Joanna Lumley's renaissance as a television actress since starring in *Absolutely Fabulous* – but what of June Whitfield, who played Edina's scatty mother? She is rarely off the radio – *The News Huddlines*, *Roundhouse*, as Agatha Christie's *Miss Marple* and now playing a Tory councillor in Radio 4's new comedy, *Any Other Business* (Wednesdays). But, she admits, "If you're not on the box, everyone thinks you're dead. *Ab Fab* just hit everybody between the eyes; I'm a born-again actress."

Does she mourn the passing of Edina and Patsy? "It's sad," she admits, "but then Jennifer [Saunders] is very astute and she's decided that this is time enough. Of course I would have liked to do another series, but I'm sure Jennifer has made the right decision. *Fawlty Towers* is back with us and they only ever made 12 episodes."

At 69, Whitfield's renaissance continues now that *Terry and June* is available on a BBC video. "It makes me laugh when people are derogatory. The fact that *Terry and June* kept going for so long must mean it had something. And the fact that so many alternative comics and critics have had a go must mean it made its mark – there's no point knocking something that nobody remembers."

June Whitfield, OBE, 50 years in showbusiness, looks unlikely to bow out. "I always say that actresses don't retire. They get retired when nobody wants to employ them any more."

Last of the summer bolly

IT WAS absolutely the last-ever fabulous episode of Absolutely Fabulous last night, and all over the country millions of distraught fans must have been consoling themselves with bottles of Bolly.

In this case, champagne might not even have been strong enough. Bring out the Stolly, girls, let's get thoroughly sloshed.

Author Jennifer Saunders is quite determined that this third series will be the last, and she's not the sort of person to have her mind changed by any amount of large cheques.

So the temptation to bring the adventures of occasional PR expert and general poseuse Edina Monsoon and her fashion editor pal Patsy to an irreversible, cataclysmic end, must have been quite a temptation.

But it was one she resisted. Instead she showed their lives apparently diverging. Patsy (the inimitable Joanna Lumley, who must go on thanking Saunders for this career boost to the end of her days) had followed tough-talking editor Magda to New York, where her ego swiftly took a bashing at the hands of new American colleagues.

Mother had become an armchair shopaholic, glued to the shopping channel, credit card ready flexed.

Edina, played by Saunders herself, was back where she began three years ago, seeking self-awareness in cultish reli-gions. But even this ridiculous chaser after trends and pretensions could see that the members of the cult were even sillier than she is. So she left in search of her true other self: selfish, cruel amoral alcoholic Patsy Stone.

The moment when Edi's helicopter came swooping down to scoop up the lonely Patsy, aimlessly wandering the New York skyline, was like so many in this priceless show. Over-the-top, ludicrous and quite touching all at once.

The episode ended by flashing forward in time 25 years to reveal Edi and Patsy still together, banished from the house by unrelenting Saffy, still drunk, still beyond the pale.

Ab Fab will undoubtedly become a TV classic, but in years to come it is not the lines we will remember, it is the images.

The long-suffering look on Julia Sawalha's dear little face, Joanna Lumley's jaw contorted into a death's head grin. And that hair. Saunders herself stuffed into silly clothes that were always too young and too small, blinking that insincere smile on and off like a beacon.

A handful of actresses throwing all dignity to the wind to show us women at their worst and give us some of the most glorious laughs of the decade.

Thanks awfully, darlings.

LAST NIGHT'S TV BY MARGARET FORWOOD

D. EXPRESS 12.3.95

Dotty mum with the girls. Above, Patsy and Eddie get jolly on the Bollie

SO WOMEN can be thick and get away with it – don't forget Jane Horrocks' Bubbles, Eddie's braindead secretary.

At last. Hurray, we don't have to be strong and sensible and self-sacrificing any more. This is fun. Now whenever we want to behave badly all we have to do is slide into Patsy and Eddie mode and the joke is obvious.

Yet however much Ab-Fab is a delicious escape, it is also riddled with uncomfortable truths about relationships between three generations of women.

For beyond Eddie's cultivated unworldliness are facets of the woman so many of us really are. She is twice divorced and feels lonely the second she is on her own. That is why she needs Patsy, her confidante who will, like her, defy encroaching age and join her for a therapeutic shopping binge. She is more solidly built than she would like to be and inevitably the lumpy bits are all in the wrong places. She knows she will never see size 10 again (or was that 12?) but she pretends to diet.

Her daughter has reached that irritating stage where she sees through her mother's pretence of being grown up.

And she understands only too cruelly that though mother is 40, or 60, or Eddie's perpetual 39, she does not actually *feel* any more grown up than she did at 18. Meanwhile, Saffy acts as though she *is* grown up by bossing Eddie around and it is Eddie who is the dependent one. Then there is Eddie's mother, played so perfectly by June Whitfield as the slightly remote granny happy to help but puzzled by the female condoms she uses as washing up gloves. "They don't put fingers in these gloves any more," she laments.

AbFab is never cosy and so you never think of it as a sitcom

IT IS, of course, and it is one of only a handful during the last 20 years that quickly became a cult and is destined to become a classic.

So, very much like the evergreen Fawlty Towers, AbFab will survive, its appeal enhanced by the wise decision to stop making TV episodes before the format became tired and stale.

On Sunday Fawlty Towers returns to BBC1 20 years after the first of its two series was shown. We must hope that 20 years from now we will still be watching Patsy and Eddie staggering hopelessly through their hazy world.

Eddie will still be screeching down her mobile phone every time she finds herself alone. Patsy will still spend her nights wrapped around young men. They will both still be drunk and oblivious to what anyone thinks of them.

And best of all, with the exception of a few frames of flash forward shown last night, they will still be 39.

Duetting with Dora

Ab Fab with Dora Bryan (opposite) – she played Mother's visiting sister who had married a GI during the war. It was fun working with Dora. I had 'followed' her a number of times in my career. *The Cure for Love*, *The Spy with a Cold Nose* and *Last of the Summer Wine* were all shows in which Dora played a part that I later inherited. Dora was magnificent as usual.

Was it the Dagger?

The first series cast of *Cluedo*, with Stephanie Beacham. Who done
it? The Reverend with the lead piping, Miss Scarlet with the revolver
or the Cook with the colander (me)?

Up your anchor for a well crewed voyage !

CARRY ON COLUMBUS

'Carry On Columbus' Queen Isabella 22,23,4,'92 (Leslie Phillips - King Ferdinand)

What a Carry On

The 1992 film *Carry on Columbus* with Leslie Phillips as King Ferdinand and me as Queen Isabella of Spain. Julian Clary introduced himself and offered me a part in an episode of his new series *Terry and Julian*. 'Oh, who am I?' I asked. 'You're the wife of the governor of the Bank of England.' 'And what does she do?' 'As a matter of fact, she tries to seduce me – now there's a challenge,' he said. How could I refuse? I then joined Julian in two series of *All Rise for Julian Clary*. I was his Auntie. He could do no wrong in his Auntie's eyes.

Panto Again with Roy

Tim would sometimes bring our dog Rabbit to the theatre and he would wait happily in my dressing room. In *Babes in the Wood* Geoff Hughes and Roy were the Panto 'robbers'. When Geoff saw Rabbit he said, 'He's just the sort of dog the robbers would have.' So Rabbit made his theatrical debut, entering with the robbers stage left and disappearing stage right. He behaved impeccably – I think he rather enjoyed it.

My dressing room. 'Elf and Safety' would have disapproved of all those wires, but a kettle, a fridge and a tiny TV are a must when two shows a day are in the schedule.

A Final Panto

1994: my last Pantomime, *Cinderella* at Wimbledon Theatre, with Rolf Harris and a great cast. (Opposite, bottom left) Nigel Ellacott and Peter Robbins as the Ugly Sisters. (Bottom right) Sally Meen, Cinderella, with her Fairy Godmother. (Above right) Ian Botham and Robin Askwith; beneath them, Rolf Harris. Living in the area I thought I'd get home between the two shows each day, but by the time I'd got home it was almost time to return to make sure of a place in the car park. After a few days I stayed in the theatre and had forty winks.

The Corner Shop

The Corner Shop in the village of Plaistow. Tim was always interested
in antiques, particularly porcelain. This delightful cottage had a shop
and Tim started a little business there. The main reason for buying
the cottage with a shop was to get away to our beloved West Sussex
at weekends. But it wasn't much of a rest, with Tim having to open
the shop. We finally decided to sell the property and Tim dealt
through various other outlets.

Travelogue

(Above) A travel advertisement for a coach company – it obviously went everywhere. (Opposite) Believe it or not, this was an advert for cheese!

June takes a seat in the Clary camp

IT is a bizarre royal coupling. Sitcom queen June Whitfield and King of Camp Julian Clary. June, 71 — Edina's mother in Absolutely Fabulous — becomes Clary's aunt for autumn's second series of All Rise For Julian Clary. The rough justice show dishes out "punishments" like dispensing condoms at nightclubs. "I hope I won't be involved in that," said June. "Past my bedtime."

Julian Clary

(Above) Julian's *This is Your Life*.
He was in Pantomime at the time,
so his *Life* was filmed in the theatre.
(Opposite) The seduction episode,
mentioned earlier, in the 1992 TV
series *Terry and Julian*.

THIS IS
YOUR LIFE

JUNE WHITFIELD O.B.E.

*This book
is presented to*

June Whitfield O.B.E.

*as a memento of her appearance
as guest of honour on*

THIS IS
YOUR LIFE

June —
your notices just get better and
better! Hope you like this one.
Love
Michael and
the team.

28th February, 1995
Thames Television, London

This is Your Life, Number 2

I was attending a dubbing session in February 1995 for *Ab Fab* with Jennifer Saunders, Joanna Lumley and Julia Sawalha, when I saw Michael Aspel approaching with 'the book'. I thought splendid, I wonder who it's for – it can't be me. When Michael said, 'This is your life', I replied, 'There must be a mistake – I've been done.' It was an even greater surprise this time. It was good to see Frank and Denis (above), who had been unable to attend the first *Life*.

It was lovely to see so many members of my family, including some younger ones, as well as so many friends (right). (Left) With my brother John and (below) with Leslie Phillips.

Dressing Up for a Publicity Shot

(Above) With Caroline Quentin and John Duttine in the radio comedy, *Kalangadog Junction*.

(Opposite) With Edward Woodward in the 1996 TV sitcom *Common as Muck*. I was his kleptomaniac girlfriend suffering from some unknown disease. My second dying role. My first was in the film of *Jude* (see following page).

✪ Common as Muck BBC1, 9.30pm

This series has proved to be a gem. Not exactly th[e]
Kohinoor diamond, but certainly a pearl among th[e]
zircons and formula Ratneresque drama output th[at]
pass for class acts these days. It's something for [which]
the BBC can rightly dust down the laurels. To the[ir]
credit (or chagrin) this tale is ending tonight. The[re will]
be no more. The writer William Ivory has deeme[d]
Common as Muck has run it's natural course. Sto[ut]
fellow. He should get a gong for Bravery in the [Face of]
Ratings with Crossed Cheques and Bar. It takes [a]
courageous man (and/or plutocrat) to kill off ch[aracters]
at the height of their popularity, but he knows [it]
has run its course. Further extrusion would simply dilute
a memorable series into latherless soap.

If only we can be assured that the BBC will not be
urging the Common as Muck ensemble to a return a la
Only Fools and Horses, whose unwelcome resurrection
is already being touted as the highlight of Britain's
Millennium celebrations. (Ten Commandments has a
ring about it. If John Sullivan had written them we'd be
up to number 732 by now – Thou Shalt Not Wear Blue
Eyeshadow or Thou Shalt Not Drop Shredded Lettuce
from Your Kebab on the Pavement on a Friday Night.)

The younger members of the …Muck cast have
performed with distinction and stalwarts such as Paul
Shane, Saheed Jeffrey, even Alexei Sayle have
conducted themselves in an exemplary manner. But
rising Duncan Ferguson-like above them all have been
Roy Hudd and Edward Woodward. Hudd has long been
a cultural hero of mine. He has proved to be inspired
casting. Woodward, his pension secured by Eighties US
crime drama rubbish, has given it his best shot – a Chris
Waddle-style swansong master class.

And if …Muck doesn't finally underline June
Whitfield's claim for a Damehood after her magnificent
contribution to radio and television over the past 40
years, then the honours system ain't worth a discarded
French fry. We don't want to miss them, but we feel
they ought to go. Common as Muck will never be
accused of outstaying its welcome. Bless 'em all.

Films for TV

(Opposite) All the way to New Zealand for fine weather to film *Jude* and of course it rained. I appeared in the Wedding Breakfast scene – I said 'Hullo' to the vicar and that was it. My cousin Verena lives in Auckland and I was able to visit her on the way there and on the way back. I had a great time meeting Kate Winslet and Christopher Ecclestone and taking a boat trip round Otago Harbour to see seals, dolphins, shags, penguins and albatrosses and their nests.

(Above) I played the pub owner Mrs Whitfield (quite a coincidence) in another TV film, *Tom Jones*. Above left with Max Beesley and, right, with John Sessions.

CBE

Another thrilling trip to the Palace. In 1998 I received my honour, a CBE – Commander of the British Empire (or Caught Before Expiry) – from Prince Charles. Wayne Sleep was also on the list and had fun nicking my hat for the photographers in the Palace courtyard, where he threw me a leg.

Chapter Nine

HANGING ON IN THERE

Bedroom Farce

Alan Ayckbourn's *Bedroom Farce* at the Aldwych Theatre in 2002, with Richard Briers, and another opportunity to work with Suzy, although in the play our characters never met.

Villains and Victims

(Top) An episode of *Miss Marple* with Greta Scacchi. I was the villain.
I am a casualty, below, in a 2004 episode of TV's *The Royals*, with Wendy
Craig as Matron.

31/08/01

EP. X.   "DELPHI"
Sc. 22.

Last of the Summer Wine

(Top left) Juliette Caplan and me as Pearl and Nelly – a
couple of bikers. In 2001, before I joined the regular cast of
Summer Wine, I appeared as a character called Delphi, who
I am playing, above, with Warren Mitchell and, left, with
Jean Ferguson and Jean Alexander.

On the Town

In this 2007 musical at the
ENO I was Madam Dilley,
the alcoholic singing
teacher. The joy of listening
to, and singing rather badly
with, a 60-plus orchestra –
magic. We shared the run
with an opera and delivered
20 performances over five
weeks. If only all theatre
was the same.

My South Bank Show

Endless trouble was taken by the producer, Nigel Wattis. He filmed me in the theatre, in Yorkshire during *Summer Wine* and unearthed material I hadn't seen for years. Melvin Bragg (with me, below) made the interviewing on the July 2007 show so relaxed and enjoyable. My thanks to everyone involved.

Green Green Grass

Her Majesty (below) attending a luncheon at RADA – she is Patron of the Academy. Timothy West looks on, with Terry Wogan on my right and Richard Briers on my left. (Left) Me as Marlene's Mum in *Green Green Grass* in 2007. I loved that role. Sadly there's no grass growing this year. I do hope it's revived.

'DORA' GREEN GREEN GRASS
10.8.07

Suzy and Terry

Suzy and her husband Terry in their garden. Various Terrys have crossed my path. Terry Scott, Terry Wogan, Terry's All Gold – it seems I will always know a 'Terry'. Suzy has married into the large Irish family Quinn, so I have inherited a whole new family. As a Mum, it's good to know that Suzy is in safe, loving hands.

Career History

1942–43 Attends Royal Academy of Dramatic Art, London

1944 Pink String & Sealing Wax – Duke of York's Theatre, London
Dear Brutus – Q Theatre, London
The Land of Promise – Q Theatre, London

1945 Little Women – Q Theatre, London
The First Mrs Fraser – repertory, Worthing
Dear Brutus & Land of Promise – tour
Appointment with Fear – tour
Pink String & Sealing Wax – Intimate Theatre, London
Fit For Heroes – tour and Whitehall Theatre, London

1946 Quiet Weekend – film, Associated British Corporation
Pink String & Sealing Wax – Penge Empire Theatre, London
The Cure for Love – tour

1947 Oak Leaves & Lavender – King's Theatre, Hammersmith and on tour
Focus on Nursing – documentary, BBC radio
Heaven & Charing Cross Road – repertory, Wolverhampton
Time & the Conways – repertory, Wolverhampton
London Dance Bands – drama-documentary, BBC radio
Cinderella – Bradford Alhambra
Wilfird Pickles' Christmas Party – BBC radio

1948 The Desert Song – tour
Cinderella – Theatre Royal, Leeds
Wilfrid Pickles' Christmas Party – BBC radio

1949 The Twenty Questions Murder Mystery – film

1950 Ace of Clubs – tour and Cambridge Theatre, London

1951 Cabaret – Studio Club, Knightsbridge
The Passing Show (popular music 1900–10) – BBC TV
Penny Plain – St Martin's Theatre, London
South Pacific – Drury Lane Theatre, London
See You Later – Watergate Theatre

1952 Women of Twilight – UK tour and Plymouth Theater, New York
Miss Hargreaves – TV play, CBS
Love From Judy – tour and Saville Theatre, London

1953 'Seven Lonely Days', 'Dancing with Someone', 'Diamonds are a Girl's Best Friend' and 'Bye Bye Baby' – records, Philips
Take it From Here – series, BBC radio

1954 Take it From Here – series, BBC radio
Fast and Loose – series, BBC TV

1955 Before Your Very Eyes – series, Associated Rediffusion TV
No Peace for the Wicked – BBC radio
Those Radio Times – BBC radio
Henry Hall's Guest Night – BBC radio

From Here and There – Royal Court Theatre, London
Star Struck – BBC radio
Man About Town – BBC radio
Bring on the Girls – BBC radio
Take it From Here – series, BBC radio
New Faces – BBC radio
Your Kind of Music – ITV
Late Show – BBC TV
Fast and Loose – series, BBC TV
Here We Go – Associated Rediffusion TV

1956 Idiot Weekly, Price 2d – series, Associated Rediffusion TV
Before Your Very Eyes – series, Associated Rediffusion TV
Take it From Here – series, BBC radio
The Tony Hancock Show – series, Associated Rediffusion TV
Curiouser and Curiouser – BBC radio
The Spice of Life – series, BBC radio
The Straker Special – musical, Associated Rediffusion TV

1957 Take it From Here – series, BBC radio
Yes, It's the Cathode-Ray Tube Show! – series, Associated Rediffusion TV
Hancock's Half-Hour, 'The Alpine Holiday' – BBC TV
The Peer's Parade – BBC radio
Chelsea at Nine – Granada TV
Before Your Very Eyes – series, Associated Rediffusion TV
Friday the 13th – BBC TV

1958 Early to Braden – BBC TV
My Pal Bob – BBC TV
Many Happy Returns – ABC TV
Dixon of Dock Green 'The Queen of the Nick' – BBC TV
Before Your Very Eyes – series, Associated Rediffusion TV
On With the Show – series, Associated Rediffusion TV
Take it From Here – series, BBC radio
Welcome to London – BBC radio
Whack-O! – sitcom, BBC TV
This is Your Life (Jimmy Edwards) – BBC TV

1959 The Army Game – sitcom, Granada TV
Murder Bag – Associated Rediffusion TV
The Army Game – sitcom, Granada TV
Carry on Nurse – film
Friends and Neighbours – film
Take it From Here – two series, BBC radio
We're in Business – sitcom, BBC radio
Whack-O! – sitcom, BBC TV
Saturday Spectacular – ITV
It's Saturday Night – BBC TV
London Lights – BBC radio

1960 Take it From Here – final series, BBC radio
Arthur's Treasured Volumes – series, ATV
The Vera Lynn Show – BBC TV
Leave it to the Boys – series, BBC radio

'Take it From Here' – record, Philips

1961 Leave it to the Boys – series, BBC radio
Beyond our Ken – BBC radio
What's the Odds – two series, BBC radio
It's a Deal – BBC radio
The Benny Hill Show – BBC TV
London Lights – BBC radio
Whack-O! – BBC TV
Variety Playhouse – series, BBC radio
The Arthur Askey Show – sitcom, ATV
Hancock, 'The Bood Donor' and 'The Radio Ham' – BBC TV
The Man in Bed – BBC TV
Juke Box Jury – BBC TV
The Seven Faces of Jim – series, BBC TV
Hancock, 'The Blood Donor' and 'The Radio Ham' – records, Pye
Does the Team Think? – BBC radio

1962 Galton and Simpson's Comedy Playhouse, 'The Telephone Call' – BBC TV
Variety Playhouse – two series, BBC radio
Whack-O! – BBC TV
Benny Hill – series, BBC TV
The Rag Trade – BBC TV
Six More Faces of Jim – series, BBC TV
Holiday Music Hall – BBC radio
Christmas Night with the Stars – BBC TV
London Lights – BBC radio
Hotel Paradiso – play, BBC TV
The Men from the Ministry – BBC radio
The Rag Trade – BBC TV

1963 More Faces of Jim – series, BBC TV
Whack-O! – series, BBC TV
Star Parade – BBC radio
Crowther's Crowd – series, BBC radio
How to be an Alien – series, Associated Rediffusion TV

1964 Steptoe and Son, 'The Bond That Binds Us' – BBC TV
Norman Vaughan – ITV
Round Trip – BBC radio
Variety Playhouse – two series, BBC radio
Baxter On... – series, BBC TV
Comedy Parade – BBC radio
The Big Noise – series, BBC TV
Starlight Hour – BBC radio

1965 Call it What You Like – series, BBC TV
This Is your Jim – series, BBC radio
Light Up the Night – BBC radio
On the Braden Beat – ATV
Porterhouse Private Eye – play, ATV
The Des O'Connor Show – ITV
Crowther's Crowd – two series, BBC radio
Not for Children – BBC radio

1966 Mild and Bitter – series, BBC TV
Frankie Howerd – BBC TV
Frankie Howerd – series, BBC radio
The Spy with the Cold Nose – film

Rikki – Scottish TV
On the Braden Beat – ATV
The Sound of Laughter – ABC TV
The Dickie Henderson Show – BBC TV
Beggar My Neighbour – Comedy Playhouse followed by series, BBC TV

1967 Life with Cooper – ABC TV
Hancock's – series, ABC TV
Beggar My Neighbour – two series, BBC TV
In Lieu of Cash – play, BBC radio
Take a Cool Look – ATV
The Young Pioneers – drama, BBC radio
Christmas Night with the Stars – BBC TV
Million Dollar Bill – BBC radio

1968 What's a Mother For? – Armchair Theatre, ABC TV
The Benny Hill Show – BBC TV
Frankie Howerd Meets the Bee Gees – Thames TV
Never a Cross Word – sitcom, LWT
Show of the Week – BBC TV
Father, Dear Father – Thames TV
The Benny Hill Show – BBC TV
Harry Worth – BBC TV
The Fossett Saga – sitcom, BBC TV

1969 The Jimmy Logan Show – BBC TV
Scott On... – series, BBC TV
According to Dora – BBC TV
The Best Things in Life – sitcom, ITV
Late Night Line Up – BBC radio
TV advertisement – Birds Eye
My Favourite Broad – play, BBC radio
Barry Humphries' Scandals – BBC TV
The Dave King Show – ATV
Frost on Saturday – LWT

1970 Scott On... – series, BBC TV
Give a Dog a Name – BBC radio
The Best Things in Life – second series, ATV
Christmas Night with the Stars – BBC TV
Do Me a Favour – sitcom pilot, LWT
TV advertisement – Birds Eye

1971 Steptoe and Son – BBC radio
Scott On... – series, BBC TV
Two's Company – BBC radio
The Dickie Henderson Show – LWT
The Dick Emery Show – BBC TV
The Magnificent Seven Deadly Sins – film
Great Scott – pilot and series, BBC radio
TV advertisement – Birds Eye
The Goodies – BBC TV
'Up Je T'Aime' – record (banned by Radio 1!)
The Val Doonican Show – BBC radio
A Tale of Two Microbes – film, Unilever

1972 The Dick Emery Show – BBC TV
Saturday Variety – ATV
The Navy Lark – BBC radio
Tarbuck's Luck – BBC TV
Commuter Tales – BBC radio
Carry On Abroad – film

Bless This House – film
Scott On... – series, BBC TV
The Frankie Howerd Show –
BBC radio
Whoops Baghdad – BBC TV
Frankie Howerd's Christmas Gala –
BBC radio
Wonderful Children's Songs – Contour
Records
A Friend Indeed – play, Anglia TV

1973 The Frankie Howerd Show – series,
BBC radio
Frankie Howerd in Ulster – BBC TV
The Dick Emery Show – BBC TV
TV advertisement – Birds Eye
Carry On Girls – film
A Bedfull of Foreigners – Victoria
Theatre, London
The Entertainers: Frankie Howerd –
BBC radio
An Evening with Francis Howerd –
series, BBC TV
The Navy Lark – BBC radio
Desert Island Discs – BBC radio
Scott On... – series, BBC TV
The Pallisers – serial, BBC TV
A Friend Indeed – TV play, Anglia TV

1974 TV advertisement – Birds Eye
Happy Ever After – Comedy
Playhouse, followed by series, BBC TV
Menace – BBC radio
The Frankie Howerd Show – series,
BBC radio
The Morecambe and Wise Show –
BBC TV
The Dick Emery Show – BBC TV
Romance With a Double Bass – film,
BBC TV
The Golden Shot – ATV
Kenneth Williams Playhouse –
BBC radio
The Val Doonican Show – ATV
Morning Story – BBC radio

1975 A Bedfull of Foreigners – South Africa
tour
Jon Pertwee's Sketchbook – BBC radio
Happy Ever After – second series,
BBC TV
A Bedfull of Foreigners – UK tour

1976 Not Now, Comrade – film
A Bedfull of Foreigners – Victoria
Palace Theatre, London
Happy Ever After – third series,
BBC TV
This Is Your Life – Thames TV
'Nursery Stories – record, Polydor
TV advertisement – Birds Eye

1977 Vivat Rex – play, BBC radio
Happy Ever After – fourth series and
Christmas special, BBC TV
This Happy Breed – BBC radio
A Bedfull of Foreigners – Hong Kong
tour
Jackanory (2 stories) – BBC TV
Pickwick Papers – serial, BBC radio
The Dick Emery Christmas Show –
BBC TV

Joint recipient of the Variety Club TV
Personality of the Year Award

1978 Weekly Ferret – pilot, BBC radio
The Lie – play, BBC radio
TV advertisement – Birds Eye
Happy Ever After – fifth series, BBC
TV
A Bedfull of Foreigners – summer
season at the Pier Theatre,
Bournemouth

1979 TV advertisement – Birds Eye
Terry and June – first series, BBC TV
'What about the Workers?' – record
Jackanory – BBC TV
Not Now, Darling – Savoy Theatre,
London

1980 TV advertisement – Birds Eye
Terry and June – second series and
Christmas special, BBC TV
It Ain't Half Hot, Mum – BBC TV
The Dick Emery Christmas Show –
BBC TV
The Basil Brush Show – BBC TV
Royal Variety Show – The Palladium,
BBC TV

1981 TV advertisement – Birds Eye
Terry and June – third series and
Christmas special, BBC TV
Mike Yarwood in Persons – BBC TV

1982 Terry and June – fourth series and
Christmas Special, BBC TV
Rupert (Bear) and the Frog Song –
cartoon, MPL Communications
Jack and the Beanstalk – Chichester
Festival Theatre

1983 Terry and June – fifth series, BBC TV
Karen Kay Show – BBC TV
Sharing Time – play, BBC TV
Tribute to Tony Hancock – BBC TV
Dick Whittington – Richmond Theatre

1984 The News Huddlines – two series, BBC
radio
It's Going to Be All Right – pilot,
Yorkshire TV
3-2-1 Pantomania – game show,
Yorkshire TV
Halls of Fame – BBC TV
The Des O'Connor Show, BBC TV

1985 Some of These Days – BBC radio
Joyful Joyce – BBC radio
The News Huddlines – two series,
BBC radio
Terry and June – sixth series, BBC TV
Jack and the Beanstalk – Theatre
Royal, Bath

1986 The News Huddlines – two series and
a Cup Final special, BBC radio
Some of These Days, BBC radio
Night of a Hundred Stars –
Shaftesbury Theatre, London
The Rivals – tour
Jack and the Beanstalk – Yvonne
Arnaud Theatre, Guildford

1987 Terry and June – seventh and final
series, BBC TV
The News Huddlines – two series,
BBC radio

An Ideal Husband – Chichester
Festival Theatre
Yesterday's Huddlines – Anglia TV
Semi Monde – The Royal Theatre,
London
1988   The Law Game – play, BBC radio
Second Chance – play, Radio Bristol
Ring Round the Moon – Chichester
Festival Theatre
The News Huddlines – two series,
BBC radio
French and Saunders – BBC TV
1989   Over My Dead Body – two-week tour
and Savoy Theatre, London
1990   It Doesn't Have to Hurt – keep-fit
series, BBC TV
Arena, special on Frankie Howerd –
BBC TV
The News Huddlines – two series,
BBC radio
Desert Island Discs – BBC radio
Hinge and Bracket – BBC radio
Babes in the Wood – Ashcroft Theatre,
Croydon
Wogan – BBC TV
1991   The News Huddlines – two series,
BBC radio
Absolutely Fabulous – pilot, BBC TV
Some of These Days – BBC radio
Pasadena Roof Orchestra – series,
BBC radio
Babes in the Wood – Theatre Royal,
Plymouth
The Craig Ferguson Story, Granada TV
1992   The News Huddlines – two series,
BBC radio
June Whitfield's Variety Special –
BBC radio
Absolutely Fabulous – first series,
BBC TV
Carry On Columbus – film
Noel's House Party – BBC TV
Terry and Julian – Channel 4 TV
Babes in the Wood – New Theatre,
Cardiff
1993   The News Huddlines – two series,
BBC radio
That's Life – series, BBC TV
Miss Marple, Murder at the Vicarage –
BBC radio
1994   The New Huddlines – two series
(including 300th edition), BBC TV
Absolutely Fabulous – second series,
BBC TV
All-Time Greats – BBC radio
The Crownded Hudds – series,
BBC radio
That's Life – BBC TV
Noel's House Party and Noel's Garden
Party – BBC TV
Cinderella – Wimbledon Theatre
The British Comedy Awards – 'Lifetime
Achievement Award'
Any Other Business – series, BBC
radio
1995   Absolutely Fabulous – third series,
BBC TV

The News Huddlines – two series,
BBC radio
Noel's House Party – BBC TV
Farewell to the Paris – BBC radio
This Is Your Life – BBC TV
Wish You Were Here – Carlton TV
All-Time Greats – BBC radio
The Crownded Hudds – series,
BBC radio
Kalangadog Junction – series,
BBC radio
Peter Pan – BBC radio
Jude – film
Gentlemen Prefer Blondes – BBC radio
1996   The News Huddlines – two series,
BBC radio
Christmas Huddlines – BBC radio
Common as Muck – BBC TV
Family Money – serial, Channel 4
Absolutely Fabulous special – BBC TV
Noel's TV Years – BBC TV
Today's the Day – BBC TV
1997   The News Huddlines – two series,
BBC radio
Christmas Huddlines – BBC radio
The Huddlines Songbook – BBC radio
Gigi – BBC radio
Tom Jones – TV film
Out of Sight – children's TV, Carlton
Get Fit with Brittas – BBC TV
All Rise for Julian Clary – series,
BBC TV
Absolutely Fabulous 'A Life' –
'documentary', BBC TV
Funny Women, featuring June
Whitfield – BBC TV
The Almost Accidental Adventures of
Bell and Todd – BBC radio
Holiday Memories – BBC TV
Going Places – BBC radio
1998   The News Huddlines – two series,
BBC radio
Christmas Huddlines – BBC radio
Friends – two episodes, NBC TV
Today's the Day – BBC TV
Loose Ends – BBC radio
The Newly Discovered Casebook of
Sherlock Holmes – series, BBC radio
Lord's Taverners Tribute Lunch
Women in Film and TV Lifetime
Achievement Award
1999   The News Huddlines – two series,
BBC radio
The Newly Discovered Casebook of
Sherlock Holmes – second series,
BBC radio
Like They've Never Been Gone – first
series, BBC radio
Timekeepers of the Millennium –
children's ITV
The Secret – drama, ITV
Hale & Pace – LWT
Days Like These – ITV
The Talkies Outstanding Achievement
Award
Inducted into the Royal Television
Society's Hall of Fame

The Last of the Blonde Bombshells – film, BBC TV

2000 Mirrorball – pilot sitcom, BBC TV
The News Huddlines – two series, BBC radio
Father Gilbert Mysteries: The Grey Lady – CD/cassette
Like They've Never Been Gone – second series, BBC radio

2001 Like They've Never Been Gone – third series, BBC radio
The News Huddlines – series, BBC radio
Absolutely Fabulous – fourth series, BBC TV
Father Gilbert Mysteries – readings, Tynedale Entertainment

2002 The News Huddlines – BBC radio
Like They've Never Been Gone – BBC radio
Bedroom Farce – Aldwych Theatre, London
Chichester Christmas Concert
Ab Fab: The Show – BBC TV
Coming Up For Air – play, BBC TV

2003 The Kumars at Number 42 – BBC TV
Graham Norton Show – BBC TV
This is Your Life (Bob Monkhouse) – BBC TV
The Seventh Floor – radio (Toronto)
Absolutely Fabulous – fifth series, BBC TV
Call My Bluff – BBC TV
BBC Worldwide trip to Jamaica
Miss Read School at Thrush Green – reading, BBC radio
The Story of Absolutely Fabulous – documentary, BBC TV
Today With Des and Mel – Carlton TV
Open House With Gloria Hunniford, Celebrity Special – Thames Television
Magazine advertisement – AXA
Carry On... – documentary

2004 Made President of TV and Radio Industries Club: TRIC

Call My Bluff – BBC TV
Bob the Builder, 'Project Build It' – BBC TV/DVD
The Royals, 'Sins of the Father' – ITV
Ab Fab About It – BBC TV
National Film Institute Evening with Sylvia Sim as interlocutor
Absolutely Fabulous Christmas Show – BBC TV

2005 Bob the Builder, 'Project Build It' – BBC TV/DVD
Last of the Summer Wine – BBC TV
Miss Marple, 'By the Pricking of My Thumbs' – Granada TV
Hitchhiker's Guide to the Galaxy – BBC radio

2006 Not Talking – play, BBC radio
Midsomer Murders, 'Midsomer Rhapsody' – ITV
Loose Ends – BBC radio
Bob the Builder – BBC TV/DVD
Last of the Summer Wine – series, BBC TV
Loose Ends – BBC radio

2007 Last of the Summer Wine – series, BBC TV
Green Green Grass – series, BBC TV
South Bank Show – ITV
Father Gilbert Mysteries, 'A Soul in Torment', 'Where the Heart Is', 'Dead Air' – Tyndale CD
On the Town – musical, English National Opera at The Coliseum
New Tricks, 'God's Waiting Room' – BBC TV
The Dinner Party – BBC radio

2008 Harley Street – ITV
Last of the Summer Wine – series, BBC TV
Green Green Grass – series, BBC TV
Kingdom – ITV

2009 Dr Who – BBC TV
Galton and Simpson's Half-Hour – BBC radio
Sexton Blake – BBC radio

Picture Credits

The images in this book have been in large part assembled from over 60 photograph and press cutting albums – the oldest, dealing with June's family, stretching back over more than 90 years. Whilst every effort has been made to trace the copyright holders, the publishers would be pleased to hear from anyone whose attribution has been missed or whose current whereabouts we have been unable to trace.

Anglia TV: 178; **Angus McBean Photograph, Copyright ©** **Harvard Theatre Collection**: 60, 61 above, 62, 63 above & below, 67; **Associated-Rediffusion**: 59, 78, 107; **Associated Television**: 148 below, 149; **Author's Collection**: 2, 4, 5 above right, 5 below left, 8, 10 (all), 11 (all), 13 (all), 14, 15, 16, 17 (all), 18 (all), 19, 20, 21 (all), 22, 23 below left, 26, 27, 28 (all), 29, 30, 31, 32 (all), 33 (all), 34 above, 35 below, 36 above, 36 below, 37 above, 39 right, 40 (all), 41, 45 (all), 46 (all), 48 (all), 49, 50 (all), 51 (all), 52, 53 above, 54, 55 (all), 56 above, 57 above, 58, 61 below, 64 below left & right, 65, 66 (all), 68 (all), 70, 71 above, 72 (all), 74-75, 76 above, 77 (all), 80 (all), 82, 84 below left and right, 87 above, 88 below, 89 below left, 90 above left, 94, 109, 111 (all), 115, 116 (all), 117 below, 119 below, 120, 121 above, 134 left, 134-35, 136 (all), 140 (all), 141, 142 (all), 143 (all), 144 (all), 145, 146 above & right, 148 above, 157, 159 below, 162 (all), 164-177 (all), 179, 181 below, 185, 186-197 (all), 198 left & below left, 199 (all), 200, 201 above, 202-207 (all), 208, 209 left, 210-216 (all), 217 below, 218 left & below, 219, 221-225 (all), 226 above right, 228-230 (all), 235, 237-256 (all), 258 (all), 260 (all), 264 above, 234 above left , 234 below right, 237-256 (all), 260 (all), 265 (all). **BBC Photographic Library**: 5 below right, 84 above, 85, 102, 119 above, 122 (all), 123 (all), 124 (all), 125 (all), 127 (all), 128, 131 above, 137, 132 (all), 133 (all), 153, 154 (all), 155, 220, 208, 261. **Bergson, Studio Jovik, Bradford**: 43, 53 below; **British Film Institute**: 103 above, 160 above right, 234 above right; **Dino Shafeek**: 180 (all), 181 above; **Doug McKenzie**: 183; **Elliott & Fry, London**: 24; **Express Newspapers**: 197 above & right; **Getty Images**: 218 above right; **Granada TV**: 232, 233 (all); **J.A.Oakley, London**: 37 below; **John Sadovy, London**: 42, 71 below, 74 above; **John Vickers, London**: 44; **J.C.E.Merry, London**: 23 (top); **Jean Weinberg, Cairo**: 23 below right; **Kaels, London**: 38, 39 left; **Marcus Adams, London**: 9; **Matthew Henderson, Bradford**: 12; **Mirrorpix**: 69, 201 right; **Parie Films, New Malden**: 25; **Pieter Toerien, Cape Town**: 64 above; **Radio Times**: 83, 113, 117 left, 118, 129, 130 below; **Rex Features**: 112, 121 below, 138 (all), 139 (all), 146 below, 147, 152, 156 (all), 160, above left & below, 161 (all), 163, 217 above, 227 (all), 257, 259 (all), 262, 263 (all), 264 below; **Star, London**: 5, above left, 91, 93 right; **Studio Briggs**: 76 below; **Swarbrick Studios, London**: 1; **T & G Reeves, London**: 34 above & below; **Unilever Films**: 158 (all); © **V&A Images/V&A Theatre Collection**: 97, 105; **Victor Mitzakis, London**: 88 above; **Western Mail & Echo**: 236.

First published in Great Britain in 2009
by Weidenfeld & Nicolson
10 9 8 7 6 5 4 3 2 1

A CIP catalogue record for this book is available from the
British Library.

ISBN: 978 0 297 85562 0

Design by Clive Hayball assisted by Tony Chung
Editorial by Ben Buchan

Colour reproduction by DL Interactive UK
Printed and bound in Italy.

Weidenfeld & Nicolson
The Orion Publishing Group Ltd
Orion House
5 Upper St Martin's Lane
London WC2H 9EA

An Hachette Livre UK Company

The Orion Publishing Group's policy is to use papers that
are natural, renewable and recyclable products and made
from wood grown in sustainable forests. The logging and
manufacturing processes are expected to conform to the
environmental regulations of the country of origin.

Mixed Sources
Product group from well-managed
forests and other controlled sources
www.fsc.org Cert no. CQ-COC-000012
© 1996 Forest Stewardship Council
FSC